PIMPETTE CHRONICLES

PIMPETTE CHRONICLES

A Modern Black Woman's Guide
To Dating Safely
& Navigating These Mean Streets

By Tinisha D. Brugnone

For information about this title, other books, or electronic media, contact the publisher.

Cinematic Griot Collective
Eastpointe, MI 48021
www.pimpettechronicles.com

ISBN
979-8-218-04345-2 (paperback)

SCAN ME

Cover and Back Design: Sean Deason
UX/UI Designer, Art Director, Graphic Designer
www.coroflot.com/seandeason

Cover and Interior Photo by Felicia Tolbert Starpointephotography

Edited By Jeffrey Wallington and Greg Dimitroff
www.starpointephotography.com

Author Headshot (back of the book)
by Tafari K. Stevenson-Howard

Interior Design: Katherine Peters
Book Formatter and Layout Designer
https://www.fiverr.com/katherine303

Dedications

To my brother, Adam Kingsley Hickman, through your death, I have become even more inspired to live. You have made me even more fearless and strong. Your strength, love, and compassion continue to empower me. Your sacrifices were not made in vain, and your story will one day be told. Because of you, failing is no longer an option. Love and light, brother! Continue to journey on.

For my cousin, Ericka (Cookie) Bellamy, your story and life continue to inspire me and so many others you crossed along the way. Flawed yet fearless, your legacy of looking out for the underdog, and protecting those who society deemed deserved no protection, helped fuel the fire that inspired me to write this book. I am my sister's keeper! Thank you for being you!

"Many of us may have been victimized, but we refuse to remain victims."

—Tinisha D. Brugnone 2022

Contents

Introduction

What makes one an authority on dating? Nowadays, we are bombarded by podcasts, self-help books, self-proclaimed social media experts, memes, and other attention-seeking sources. Many are not designed or interested in addressing the challenges of everyday Black women living in the average Black, or if you prefer, African American community. These influencers rarely acknowledge how diverse many of our social, economic, and cultural differences are, and their perspectives may not fit into your reality.

Modern mainstream media often presents unrealistic expectations of what a compatible partner may look like in your own community. Since some believe there are severe shortages of "eligible" Black men for reasons which include: mass incarceration, homosexuality, unemployment, or underemployment. Black women (no matter what their socioeconomic status) are left chasing behind the same handful of what our communities may consider a "catch."

First, let's acknowledge that communities and how they define an "eligible man" are as diverse as everyone. Some of us may come from a southern-rooted background, while others may have more northern influences. Even in today's society which is deeply impacted by the things we consume virtually, where we live ultimately affects how we choose our mates.

With these facts and others, this book is most suitable for women living in the Midwest area or any major predominantly Black neighborhood or big city across the US. It is also the author's belief that this book could be used anywhere there is a higher woman-to-man ratio in the United States. Although this book is written from the perspective and views of a Black Woman, it can be useful to any woman who has found herself stumbling while dating during the COVID-19 pandemic and its aftermath.

The purpose of this book is to provide the average hetero- or bisexual woman with a basic guide to help ensure that she can navigate through the dating world with clarity, knowledge, safety, confidence, and most importantly, **POWER**. This book flows from the experiences and beliefs of the author, sometimes juxtaposed, or aligned with the beliefs of her peers, community, matriarchs, grandparents, aunts, uncles, etc. The stories and characters are fictional, and any similarities to real persons are coincidental. This book is also supported by research and development done by scholarly sources et al. As these groups and elders have professed, "The players change, but the game stays the same."

About the Author

Tinisha Brugnone is an African American Creative born and raised in Detroit, Michigan. She has a Bachelor's degree in Media Arts and Studies, with a concentration in Production, from Wayne State University. She has also graduated with honors from the School of Hard Knocks.

Ms. Brugnone, a storyteller and award-winning Director/ Producer/Screenwriter, is the curator of the Idlewild International Film Festival, a woman-centered festival that highlights filmmakers internationally. She has been featured in many news outlets, including NPR's Michigan Public Radio, The Detroit Free Press, and Metro Times. Tinisha currently works as a freelance filmmaker, having landed positions and gigs with media sources such as "Now This," "ABC Foreign News Correspondent," "PBS," and many more.

Tinisha has more than 30 years of dating experience, including several long-term committed relationships. Most recently, venturing back into the dating scene, she has emerged from those past experiences with a greater understanding of love, respect for herself and her mate, and ultimately, **POWER**. After years of inner work and healing, she has gained the insight, clarity, and confidence required to curate the type of life she wants. She believes this book will help her readers do the same.

Respectfully, Tinisha's advice does not come from a foundation of Christianity. However, she grew up attending church and adds that if any belief system were the foundation, it would be that of a spiritual one. She further has stated that she doesn't believe in "one true soulmate," staying in unfruitful or abusive relationships, living for others, or denying oneself the most basic and innate rights as a woman, which include: the right to be loved, protected, adored, and respected.

This book is written from a seasoned mature Black Woman's perspective whose intent is to share her wisdom, knowledge, and experience. This is not a "how to get a man" book; instead, it is a reference guide on how to date and reduce the possibility of harm to yourself and others. Lastly, Tinisha writes this book with the hopes that other women can benefit from her blunt honesty, humor, and insight. P.S. This is not your momma's dating guide.

Chapter 1

The Paradigm Shift

W hen I was a little girl, I often heard that the world was coming to an end. I'd stay up late wondering if I would live to see the next morning. Even as a young woman, I would become uneasy whenever the next self-proclaimed prophet would start with the warnings. I am embarrassed to say that I was completely terrified and convinced the world was ending on New Year's Eve 1999. After all, Prince had even made a song about it.

I have since learned not to believe everything I hear, even when it comes from what appears to be a reputable source. Instead, I now let my intuition lead me to this freeing feeling that has left me with so much clarity. The more I have allowed myself to be led by my own intuition, the more successful I have become in my endeavors.

I've often heard that the new millennium is the millennium of the woman. Some even believe that women will rule for the next 1,000 years. Judging by the fact that the United States has its first "Black"

Woman Vice President, and just recently, the U.S. Supreme Court confirmed Ketanji Brown-Jackson as our first Black Woman Justice, my intuition tells me that this will come to pass but probably not in my lifetime and definitely not without some real and immediate change.

The growing leadership of women is not just apparent in the U.S. but also in many other countries around the world. Since men have done such an awesome job at ruling the world—[insert sarcasm here]—it is only fitting that the ladies be given the same opportunity. Until most recently, for the first time in modern history, women had more control over their bodies, reproduction, and finances, garnering the right to pick and choose who they mate with and ultimately bear children by. As a result, lawmakers have been on a mission for decades to roll back reproductive rights, and with the reversal of Roe vs. Wade for Black Women, these changes will create even more challenges for our communities.

As Black women being forced to assimilate into a patriarchal society, we often fall victim to the rules and government that are most likely foreign to the core of some of our DNA. I use the word "some" because we are mixed people from various ethnic groups that were kidnapped from our motherland. Science has already proven that DNA has memory. I suspect there are valid and numerous reasons why we clash with our males when they attempt to dominate us.

For one, history has revealed that many political systems in pre-capitalist Africa were either matriarchal or matrilineal, so it simply does not always feel natural for us to "blindly" follow behind our men, which may explain the constant turmoil many of us find ourselves in. Not to mention that not all men are equipped to lead, but I digress…. That is a conversation for another book.

In addition to our souls dealing with memory, Black men in the United States hold so little power it is no surprise that they are grasping at the power that they hold over their women. Many are perfectly comfortable with claims of wanting to empower Black people but then turn a blind eye to the things they do to de-power the Black woman. Resistance is futile, or is it?

While discussing what can be described as a "paradigm shift," Detroit-based community organizer Kwasi Akwamu stated the following: "There has been a significant change in gender relations for some years now. When society began to open up to greater participation of women, it created a shift in the self-awareness of the women, greater confidence, goal-centeredness, and a form of independence that didn't neatly fit the traditional paradigm men are taught.

A greater number of men are stuck in a state of confusion, being unable to relate to the new woman who lacks the shackles of dependency. Some applaud, and others shrink in fear of their ability to meet her as an equal. Women are not always gentle in asserting their new aspirations, freedoms, and state of dependence. Ultimately, we must rediscover one another on new terms, respecting and learning one another as whole human beings who select companions on a fresh set of terms. And lastly, we must overcome the diseased influences of this society which compromises and commodifies our relationships. Social media contributes significantly to the dysfunction of our present-day relationships."

Indeed. Social media has deeply contributed to how we view relationships and each other. Relationships are not valued partly because many of us feel like our mates are easy to replace. In public, we look for ways to appear to have it all together in hopes of gaining the approval of our peers, whether real or virtual, but we seldom work as hard at keeping our mates happy.

With all the challenges we experience while living in this Matrix and our new reality, it has become difficult to meet and connect with a partner. Most people are entirely too preoccupied, selfish, and distracted to skillfully face the task of focusing on one person at a time.

Often we start with high hopes, and as soon as that person does not fit into our agenda, we quickly move on. It is clear that relationship goals and priorities will never be as they were decades ago, and in some regard, that is definitely a good thing. To embrace our new reality, we must have a new objective. As Modern Black

Women living in the United States, it is our time to move ourselves toward a position of **POWER.**

Am I Ready to Date?

I know you are gorgeous, sexy, and confident, and any man would be lucky to have you, but before one can make herself available to a potential mate, you must first ask yourself, "Are you dateable?" before you ask, "is he?" This is the time to take a good, honest look at yourself to ensure that you have dealt with or are dealing with your issues in a way that will not affect the potential relationship.

As women, we are good at looking at a man to decide whether or not "he" is worth our attention, but how many of us first look in the mirror? There are some basic things that all men with any minute amount of common sense will look for in a potential long-term mate, and for you to ensure that you are always treated like a priority instead of an option, let's make sure that you have them.

Do I Have a Steady Income or Source of Money?

Did you know that most men prefer that their potential mates have some source of income when they meet and throughout the courtship? This shows that a woman can take care of the household if they were ever to become a family if he is not able to for whatever reason. This also balances out the power dynamics in the relationship. Some believe that men respect women more when they aren't completely reliant on them.

There are, of course, exceptions to the rule as the relationship progresses more toward a family. But in this book, the focus remains on the dating stage while touching on the beginning aspects of being in a partnership. For our purposes, we are examining relationships from a traditional household where the man will usually become the breadwinner.

We understand that all households function differently, but even in today's modern society, most men, when asked, enjoy being able to provide for their partner and, eventually, his family. Only those unable to do so are usually the ones to seek mates wishing to share 50/50 of the expenses. Please keep in mind that studies continue to show that, even when a woman works outside the home, the bulk of the household chores and raising of the children will fall on the mother.

Am I Emotionally Mature?

Sadly, too many of us have grown up in households where we have experienced situations where emotional or physical abuse has occurred at least on one occasion. I know this is an ugly topic, and no one likes to talk about it, let alone read about it, but the shit is real. It would be a huge disservice if we were to dismiss this common relationship problem as if every companionship was going to be filled with rainbows and butterflies.

These abusive relationships are brought on by the inability to resolve conflict in a healthy way, which could erupt in physical abuse on either end. Remember, women can be, and often are, abusers, too. Although the cases where women abuse men are significantly less in comparison, we must still acknowledge that the pendulum swings both ways.

To reduce the likelihood of you being the catalyst in a domestic dispute, here are some things to ask yourself before you meet Mr. Right:

- How do I react to conflict?

- Do I yell or scream?

- Do I think it is normal or OK to call a man out of his name or belittle him when I am angry?

- Do I hit or throw things at people?

- Do I have trouble controlling my temper or emotions in a way that can become dangerous to myself and others?

- Do I enjoy emasculating or attacking his manhood?

- How do I react when my feelings are hurt?

- Is my first reaction to strike back?

- Do I simply withdraw and run away from the person?

- How do I react when he shows emotion?

- Am I usually dismissive, or can I be attentive?

If you find yourself thinking Yes, when you should be thinking No, this is the time to confront and correct those bad habits before you meet and chase away a potential good catch. At no stage in life will any of us ever be perfect, but the goal is to strive to be the **best versions of ourselves** so that we can be a gift, not a curse, to our future mates. Below are some indications that you are emotionally mature:

- You discuss your feelings in a calm, mature way, as well as listen to him.

- You can express how you feel, give the other person a chance to remediate the issue, and allow for forgiveness depending on the severity of the offense.

- You do not bring up past mistakes once they are confronted and dealt with.

- You are open, honest, and do not intentionally play games with emotions or feelings.

- You do not, under any circumstances, ever intentionally emasculate his manhood or throw anything in his face that he has shared with you in confidence.

- You can walk away if you see that you are not on the same page as he is without attacking his character or point of view. *Yes, sometimes you will need to throw that fish back in the pond, no matter how tasty it may be.*

On paper, this all sounds simple, but in practice, it may be hard for some while easy for others. If you find yourself stepping out of character, it's OK to take a break and return to a discussion or issue later when you are calm and clear-headed. Just calmly let your partner know that you would like to revisit at another date. Assure him that you are not avoiding but are not in the state of mind required to objectively address the problem. Remember, sometimes, the way that we handle things as women, are affected by our menstrual cycle and hormones. If you notice you are becoming moody or easily angered, check the dates on your period tracker to see where you are and log the emotions.

After a while, you may see a pattern. For older ladies who are peri/premenopausal or menopausal, constantly work to keep yourself in check since hormones fluctuate erratically during this time. Be mindful that some male companions will use the knowledge of how our hormones work, as an excuse for being dismissive or disrespectful. I am not bringing this up to suggest that you silence yourself or allow yourself to be silenced, but to simply acknowledge that we are all still just mammals and our biological functions affect every aspect of our lives, including how we communicate. Please note that most men, no matter how old, will sometimes behave like spoiled, little mannish boys, so always maintain your composure. Be cool, yet speak firmly when putting a brotha in check.

Exhibit A: Trisha and Malik have been dating for over two months. Malik constantly compliments her on her figure and is extremely attracted to her. One day, while out and about, Malik gropes Trisha on her ass in a way that makes her feel uncomfortable, mainly because they are out in public, and secondly, they have not built that level of affection yet. Trisha took a deep breath and calmly told Malik that she doesn't like to be touched that way and asked him how he would feel if a man his daughter was dating did that to her. Malik immediately apologized and never did it again.

Trisha's first instinct was to tell him off. This was partially because it was just a few days before her cycle, and experience had taught her to be extremely careful of how she expresses herself during this time. At that moment, she had to quickly decide whether or not she wanted to use this scenario as a teachable moment or enjoy the temporary satisfaction of gut-punching that ass! Be aware that some men will test your boundaries (intentionally or not) to see how you respond to certain behaviors. Trisha made a conscious decision in her life to always remain in control yet still express how she felt when disrespected. In her experience, control equated to **POWER.**

Have I Done My Inner-Work?

Inner-work can be described as the internal journey to explore your inner self to understand, heal, and finally, transform.

Nowadays, everyone is talking about being spiritual and doing their inner-work, which is wonderful and well overdue, to say the least. After all, we are in what can only be described as a **paradigm shift** in how men and women relate to each other, amongst other things. Being proactive instead of reactive is key to navigating safely through these streets. As most of us are learning, the probability of conflict arising between the sexes is more likely than not these days. With that in mind, it has become increasingly important that we protect our peace and only allow men who are positive and nurturing to become and stay a part of our personal lives.

When we have sex and become intimate, we are undoubtedly at our most vulnerable state of being. For this reason, it should not be taken lightly. No matter your belief system, one must acknowledge that we are all made up of energy, which can be exchanged but never destroyed. With that basic notion, avoiding negative energy is vital to your overall well-being.

For example, have you ever noticed that you would feel sad or angry if you go around an angry or negative person or place? Or how you feel somewhat uplifted when you are around a positive or happy person.

Remember, we are living in perilous times, and death and destruction have been running rampant since COVID-19 began to sweep across the world. To scroll through our social media and not see an obituary or someone saying they have lost a loved one is rare. Suicide and murder cases are growing, and it is important that we work toward maintaining a healthy and balanced life and protect ourselves. This includes being mindful and observant of the type of energies (aka people) we allow into our personal space. This will ensure that you are always vibrating on a positive frequency.

Here are some tips that can help you in doing your inner-work and assure that you are one of the types of positive people you want to attract:

- Confront your past pains. This includes feelings of self-doubt, past romantic relationship issues, familial relationships, fear of abandonment, inadequacies, sexual issues, addictions, whether drugs or food, and body image.

- Develop healthy habits that make you feel good about yourself. This may include some sort of physical activity. Try waking up every morning and committing to an hour of exercise, or maybe do it at the end of your day. Whatever time is best, just know that any aerobic activity will help you feel strong and empowered. It doesn't matter what you commit to, as long as it is good for you and makes you feel good.

- Watch what you put into your body. Have you heard the saying, "You are what you eat?" Well, this is truer than a lot of us want to admit. Putting healthy foods and drinks in your body helps you remain focused and keeps you feeling energetic throughout your day.

- Acknowledge your past pains and forgive yourself for your mistakes. Often, we forgive others but fail to forgive ourselves.

- Ask for forgiveness if you have done something wrong and it is heavy on your heart, if it is safe to do so. This does not mean the victim has to forgive you, but you can still release that negative energy and forgive yourself. From there, you should move on. Some people may prefer to write down the transgression and burn it to release it into the atmosphere. The choice is yours.

- Thank the universe, your god, yourself, or whomever for teaching you the lessons you have learned and will continue to learn throughout your life journey.

- Practice daily affirmations. For example, a daily routine that includes saying aloud, "I am a good person, and good things will come to me."

- Put a white dry-erase board in your home where you can write reminders to be gentle and kind to yourself and acknowledge your strengths, needs, wants, goals, and accomplishments.

- Think about your intent and the person you want to be, and develop a life plan.

- Seek counseling. If you have not begun your healing journey and are dealing with grief, pain, or other challenges, please seek professional help before you begin or continue dating.

Do I Have My Own Interests, Hobbies, and Friends?

Before we open ourselves up to let someone come into our lives, we must ensure that we have our own life, which should include a series of activities we enjoy. Men are often inspired and amazed by women who have their own thing going on, especially those who continue to do what they enjoy, whether he is around or not. Continue to hang out with your friends, but only if you have healthy relationships with those friends. Don't cancel your ballroom classes or stop attending book club meetings. Don't skip out on game night or stop visiting your parents on Sundays.

Mature and emotionally-available men trying to get to know you enjoy hearing about the things you are enthusiastic about and the people you love. The key is to maintain balance while keeping your life on track, especially while dating. Have a hobby, no matter how big or small, and stick with it. Trust me; you do not want to appear like you have nothing you feel passionate about when meeting someone new. Remember to continue investing time in the relationships you have already built with friends and family, even after finding a suitable mate. Sometimes our romantic relationships do not work out, and it would not be wise to alienate yourself from the shoulder you may need to cry on.

Am I Certain of the Things I Do Not Want?

It's an exciting time in the world for women simply because we have the power to choose. Never let anyone convince you that you are limited or you do not have options. The key to having options is positioning yourself in a position of **POWER** and being strategic. Create a chart similar to the one below and be as detailed as possible. Remember, we may all want a dude with a six-pack who is making six figures, but do we have a six-pack, or are we making six figures? Of course, opposites sometimes attract but let's try to be realistic in our expectations.

Pimpette Chronicles

To help you get started, here is an example chart:

Requirements and/or Desires in a Mate	Absolute YES	Absolute NOT	Maybe	Bonus
Income Above $80,000 per year	✔			
College Educated			✔	
Christian Faith		✔		
No Children Under 18		✔		
African American Natural Born Male	✔			
Drinks Alcohol			✔	
Goal Oriented				✔
Monogamous				✔
Bisexual		✔		
Wants Children	✔			
Loves Animals				✔
Physically Handsome			✔	
Muslim Faith	✔			
Erect Penis Size Over 6 inches			✔	
Uses Profanity		✔		
Spiritual		✔		
Sexually Healthy/No Erectile Dysfunction	✔			

The Paradigm Shift

Requirements and/or Desires in a Mate	Absolute YES	Absolute NOT	Maybe	Bonus

Requirements and/or Desires in a Mate	Absolute YES	Absolute NOT	Maybe	Bonus

While dating and making yourself available for potential mates, you will often find yourself adding and subtracting from your list of requirements and desires. If you want to get deeper, consider adding points based on the importance of each category to you. For example, the things that are Absolute YES can be 5 points, and the Nos could be 0s. This will give you a point system to rate your potentials by.

The entire reason for dating is to get to know what you want and need in a mate. As we continue to evolve and mature, those needs and wants change, which is perfectly normal. Most of us will not require the same thing at 26 that we will at 46, so don't let others convince you that you are fickle or don't know what is best for you. Remember, the most important thing is knowing what you **DO NOT** want in your life and not accepting it into your world.

Am I Dateable?

According to any dictionary, "dateable" simply means being attractive in a romantic way. With that in mind, it is safe to say that some men are willing to "date" almost anyone. What this means to you as a woman is that you must constantly be on the lookout for wolves in sheep's clothing, that is, "IF" you are looking for a mate. If you are not, that's cool, too. This book will still serve you well.

I want you to understand that some men will intentionally date you for months or years and have no intention of ever committing to you. Most men know exactly what type of woman they want, and you may not even be in the running. It has absolutely **NOTHING** to do with how beautiful you are, how sexy you are, how wholesome you are, how intelligent you are, how well you cook, and it's definitely not about how well you put it down in the bedroom!

Have you ever noticed how some men can be with an intelligent, beautiful, sexy woman and then turn around and marry the most basic chicks? This is partly because, since boyhood, men have developed an idea of what they want their wife to be like, even though many men lack the emotional maturity needed to choose wisely. You may even run into mature men, who still think like boys, who are searching based on some standard embedded in them (by a previous generation of dysfunctional men) that either does not exist or they themselves cannot live up to. This contributes to why most marriages end in divorce. Contrary to popular belief, it may not even have anything to do with whether they "love" you or not.

Also, be aware that some men will attempt to put you in a category and expect you to stay there for the rest of your life. In all honesty, some of these categories may even be beneficial to you, but it is **YOU** who should determine what role you allow yourself to play and just how long you want to play it.

Chapter 2

Asset or Liability?

W e live in an era where people are more comfortable with lies than with the truth. Some of us are in denial about who we are and what makes us an asset or a liability. We yell body positivity, but we ignore the fact that according to the CDC, obesity-related illnesses, such as heart disease, are the leading cause of death amongst African Americans. With the current health crisis, we simply cannot discuss dating and choosing a mate without acknowledging that who we choose as a partner influences all aspects of our lives, including our finances, emotional well-being, and health.

With that in mind, remember that dating someone who eats unhealthy means that you are more likely to start or continue eating unhealthily. If that person becomes ill due to their poor eating habits, you may end up responsible for their care, which could be taxing and costly. Being reliant on someone emotionally, physically, or financially can put you (or the other person) at a disadvantage in the relationship. Also, if you cannot properly care for yourself, your partner may start to look at you as a burden and treat you as such.

Think about reality TV, for instance, where we have witnessed cases where individuals who were morbidly obese had to miss out on certain activities because the space could not accommodate them. This keeps the couple from enjoying life to the fullest and often limited in what they can enjoy. Not to mention the caregiver, often the mate, usually remains worried from wondering if the person they love will die from their condition. This is not a situation anyone should want to go into, knowing it may be an issue. Being mindful that what you do can affect your future mate should make you want to be the **best version of you.** Not saying you have to be perfect but keep working toward your health and life goals even while dating.

In cases of finances, without adequate income, your potential mate may feel pressured to come in and rescue you in the event of an emergency. Depending on how long you have been dating, they may opt out of the relationship in fear of their own resources being drained. In some cases, the desire to combine households may develop prematurely just to keep the relationship going. Best case scenario, you should have your own money, which inevitably equates to **POWER,** and be able to take care of yourself. Even if your cash flow is limited, the potential mate does not need to know and probably won't notice.

Asset or Liability?

Realistically, most women are aware that some men (over a certain age) are accustomed to coming in and fixing a woman's situation. They may feel completely useless if you do not require that they fix yours. Those men generally have their entire self-esteem wrapped up in materialistic things, and this sort of mindset may not be ideal for many reasons. For instance, if the relationship fails, the first thing the "sponsor" wants to do is remind you how much they have done for you and how you would be nowhere without them. Men who like to be a "captain save a hoe" will often use their financial status to control the women in their lives. They have no problem throwing the things that they did for you in your face at a time that is convenient for them.

In partnership, the goal is to work together and have skills that complement each other. No one should enter with the notion of having to fix someone else's life completely. When you are stable in your own life, of course, the man who cares for you will want to make your life better. So even if your credit is fair, instead of good, most men will not look at you as a liability as long as he sees that you have taken steps to work toward bettering your situation. A really good catch will even step in to help you reach your financial goals because they understand that most people will endure some sort of financial hardship in their lives, so that alone would not make you a liability. What determines whether or not you are an asset is your potential and overall value in the relationship. Wise men will see the total package and assess from there.

Becoming the Best Version of You!

"Every woman has something beautiful about her, but every woman ain't beautiful!" – Drunk Auntie, Circa 1990

During the 1980s, colorism in the Black community (and many other POC communities) ran as rampant as it does today. In some communities, it is not uncommon to hear men stating a preference for light-skinned women over dark-skinned ones. We hear it in our music and see it every time we turn on the television and see a mixed-race light-skinned woman representing "Black Women." Although I am a mother of two fairly light Afro-Latina women, I can still fully see and acknowledge the misrepresentation and attempt at erasure of the beauty of Black women who carry the darker shades of brown.

Personally, it is a constant reminder that the more things change, the more they stay the same. I still remember times as a child when I would cry to my grandmother, believing I was ugly because I had full lips and dark skin. I can recall when my older siblings and older cousins would argue over who had the darker skin, me or my cousin. Experiences like this ultimately affect our perspectives of beauty, and we carry this trauma into adulthood, whether we know it or not.

Asset or Liability?

The challenges of seeing oneself as beautiful are not limited to just Black women, nor women of a darker shade of brown. On the contrary, women of all hues often speak of their feelings of inadequacy. Some of us may worry about the size of our breasts or our weight. At the same time, others struggle with their hair, lips, and even the shape of their legs.

As a result, nowadays, many women are flocking to get breast implants, Brazilian butt lifts, nose jobs, or any other procedure that may garner the attention and approval of others. Since cosmetic surgery should be considered extreme and a last resort, there are other ways to make a sista feel like the queen that she is, and it starts with the "inner-work" mentioned in the previous chapter.

Once we have ensured our traumas are in check, we can move forward with our exterior. This can be as simple as choosing clothing that fits and accentuates our best attributes or developing a fitness regime that keeps us feeling our best while maintaining a comfortable weight and size. Most women with a basic level of self-esteem have something they love about themselves. A friend of mine loves her feet, so she often chooses open-toed shoes.

If you have great legs, show those off! One thing about a nice set of legs is that some men will follow them anywhere, and most won't even care what the face looks like. Another friend loves her bosom, so she purchases a lot of low-cut blouses. As for me, I am proud of my derrière, so it's not uncommon to see me in a form-fitting sweater dress in the winter or a nice sundress in the summer. Booyah!

Before choosing your clothing, be honest with yourself about how the garment looks on you, and only wear items that you will feel confident and comfortable in. Don't choose exclusively based on designer labels or what's in. Select colors and cuts that accentuate your body, complexion, and undertone. It is no secret that everyone likes to feel sexy and powerful from time to time, and clothes can be tailored to fit our moods, environment, and situation.

For those who believe in age-appropriate sexiness, please remember that what looks good on one person will not automatically look good on another. With this in mind, we need to carefully consider our bodies and choose garments that bring out the best in us without making us look sleazy or sloppy.

Here are some of my rules of thumb, but remember to always choose what you feel works for you, and use this only as a guide:

- When the garment has a low-cut top, stick to pants or a mid-to longer length dress or skirt.

- If the top, shirt, or blouse has a high collar and does not show cleavage, you can be a little riskier with a mini skirt or shorts.

- If the dress is extremely form-fitting, make sure it is medium to long in length. Nothing sexy about pulling your dress down all the time.

- If the dress is super short and has a completely covered bosom, put on a pair of thigh-high boots to compensate for the lack of material elsewhere.

- If the garment is sheer and risky, choose a fit that's a little loose, never extremely tight. As a middle-aged woman, I often choose a full coverage two-piece or a one-piece body or bathing suit. For younger ladies, you can choose a thong or string bikini top "if" you feel comfortable in it.

Please keep in mind where you are going when choosing your looks. You are not going to wear clubwear to the church and vice versa. No matter what, when you step out of the house, ensure you are fresh and clean. If you were taught growing up about wash-ups and hoe baths, let that shit go! No grown-ass person should be taking either of these unless they do not have access to a shower or bath; it is simply not acceptable.

Remember to always keep a casual outfit ready if you are on the go a lot. Make sure your hair is washed and smelling good at all times. Invest in dry shampoo if you are into wigs or braids, etc. Most of us natural girls and braid-wearers must wash our hair a minimum every three weeks, so don't wear that style if it looks or smells dusty and old.

Your mate will often grow accustomed to your smell, so make sure you have your signature fragrance that will always be familiar.

For example, while dating a more nature-centered guy, I noticed that he loved when I wore Amaretto fragrant shea butter, so I always wore it when he was around. While dating a guy who was more of a capitalist, I would spray myself with expensive perfumes when I knew I would see him. My theory is the first guy was more connected to nature, which is why natural smells appealed to him, while the other guy was more interested in wealth, so expensive smelling (and looking) women appealed more to him.

Also, avoid high heels if you cannot confidently walk in them. In this day and age, a tutorial can help you master those. When a confident woman walks, she should be strolling like that chick in the Michael Jackson video, *Thriller!* The wrong pair of shoes can mess up your entire game plan. Believe me when I say people love to see a woman who will turn heads when she walks into a room, and it's all in how she carries herself. If you are new to the game, don't be afraid to practice your walk, and own it, sis!

Once you are on that date, always be polite to the wait staff, and if your order is wrong, calmly explain without making a scene or becoming obnoxious. Nobody wants to be out with the hoodrat who will be the cause of the waiter putting a booger in their food. I cannot stress this enough. Some women seem to think the snotty behavior is cute, but grown men will never go out with you again for this reason alone. Number one complaint I've heard from them.

Asset or Liability?

Keep in mind, if you want to be seen as a classy chick, read up on basic dining etiquette. It's shocking how many women aren't taught basic things, such as putting their napkins on their laps, keeping their elbows off the table, and chewing with their mouths closed. Also, remember to say thank you at the end of the evening. Men will absolutely judge you on this and assume that you are not grateful. Even though we know he should thank you for gracing him with your presence, it is still common courtesy and good character to show appreciation.

Additionally, if possible, please invest in at least one piece of fine jewelry if you do not own any. When men see that you are used to nice things, they will want to give you nice things. He doesn't have to know that you bought it, or if you want to further show that you can provide for yourself, you can share that info if it comes up. Just remember that men are always in competition and will often try to outdo each other, so a little mystery is wise, too.

Lastly, if you have had a bad relationship in the past, keep that shit to yourself. The men you date are not your therapist. Best practice is to not reveal those details until after you are married or close to it. Maybe not even then. So, as far as he should know, every man has treated you well, but it just did not work out because you grew apart. Finally, never tell a man about a bad experience with an ex and then ask him not to do the same. It is almost certain that he will. Trust me, it never fails.

How Do You Feel?

If you Google the term "body positivity," you will learn that there are numerous descriptions and definitions of this term. Some sources state it is a movement that encourages you to accept the things you cannot change about your body and was established with persons with disabilities in mind. Other sources say it is a movement to eradicate beauty standards and what is considered attractive and what is not.

Whatever description we agree with, the question we should ask ourselves is, how do we feel, and what is our overall health? If your body feels like something that is weighing you down, limits what you can do physically, full of pain, discomfort, or if it is causing illnesses such as diabetes, heart disease, high blood pressure, etc., then the first step is to address those issues. No amount of yelling body positivity is going to change the fact that our lifestyles and diet affect every single aspect of our lives, including how we move, date, and choose a mate.

It is a challenge for most of us to take control of our health and diet, and many struggles every day. My weakness is that I absolutely love to snack, so regularly, I enjoy high-calorie, high-fat foods such as potato chips and fries. My weight fluctuates, and since I don't believe in dieting, I practice eating in moderation, exercise, and work to eliminate and reduce the foods that are not good for me. This is because I know my body and can feel when I have not been treating her well.

The truth is that we only get one, so we should treat it kindly, which includes helping it stay strong through aerobic activity and putting foods rich in vitamins and nutrients in it that will help keep her healthy and youthful. Yes, beauty comes in all shapes and sizes, and how a person looks does not determine whether or not they are healthy, this is certain. But, the truth is, if you go to the doctor regularly, you know what your health is and what you need to do to be **the best version of you.**

Oftentimes when we are young, we will feel great with no issues. Just keep in mind that as we age, we all begin to deteriorate (no matter our size), so you want to make sure you can continue to move without pain. Do you think the older lady with a walker ever saw herself being reliant on such a device, or the person on the scooter at the grocery imagined that ride in their future? Some things are beyond our control but know that excess weight puts pressure on our joints, and many times, the pressure causes pain.

Many people I knew who had unhealthy diets or were inactive in their 20s now have knee replacements, high blood pressure, diabetes, etc., in their 40s. If I stop working out for a month, I will immediately start having back pains. Bad eating habits and lack of movement catch up with us all, no matter our size, so it's important to be proactive so that we can feel good in our skin and age gracefully. For this and other reasons, always try to date persons who share similar beliefs about health as you do (assuming you care about your overall health) so that you can encourage each other. If you meet someone who doesn't care about what they eat, you may be able to influence them to change their habits, or they may influence you in the opposite direction.

I only date men who are mindful of what they put in their body and how they treat it. By dating in this manner, it allows me to stay on track with my own health regimen. Since I do not like to eat much fast food, I no longer date men who eat it often. Since I enjoy working out, I am attracted to men who enjoy some sort of aerobic activity, even if it is just walking regularly or riding their bikes. This also gives us something to do together and helps build a bond. Most of us nowadays work sedentary jobs, so it is even more important to be intentional with caring for our bodies and health. When making relationship choices, I recommend you choose persons who will work with you toward all your life goals, not those who will make them harder to achieve.

Raising Your Own Net Worth

We live in a society where absolutely everyone is being judged. People often form an opinion of you before you even open your mouth. Folks will size you up based on the type of car you drive, how you dress, your profession, and even what type of background you come from. With the advent of social media, people who have never met you in real life get an idea of who you are based on how much or little you share.

Most of us have become characters in this metaverse, a world far from authentic. It's a sad inescapable truth that few will admit. For those of us who choose, or are forced, to navigate societal norms and be a part of this weird new realm of reality, we also have to make adjustments to survive and thrive. As Black babies of African descent born in the United States, we literally came into this earth at a disadvantage. Add being a woman, growing up in the inner city where you more likely have spent most of your life operating in survival mode, and it's no surprise that many of our romantic relationships fail. These facts must be considered even while dating.

As mentioned previously, men know exactly what type of woman they want to settle down with, which means that no amount of appearing to be perfect on social media or in person is likely to change that. Nowadays, we are encouraged to seek out likes and mentions, but please remember that sharing too much on social media can actually damage your dating experiences. I believe leaving some things to be learned only by a potential mate is the best practice. I normally do not date anyone with who I am connected on social media, or if I am, I change the settings to keep them from knowing "everything" I choose to share. When we meet up, they can find out what I had for lunch or my review of the play I just saw.

In addition, in this day and age, it is advantageous for us as women to always strive to empower ourselves and the people around us. Empowerment comes in many forms, including maintaining balance and harmony in your life, educating yourself, and striving toward financial security. Make a list of things you feel will make you a stronger, more confident, knowledgeable person. Set an attainable goal, and work toward achieving it, slowly but surely.

As an example, one of the things that I have always wanted to learn is belly dancing, so I have recently started taking classes. Not that I necessarily want to be a performer or even share my skills with the world, I just want to learn for my friends, myself, and possibly my future mate. How exciting would it be for him to one day experience me in my costume, using my veil in an enticing way? It is also great exercise and helps keep me working toward my health goals. Another skill that I have acquired over the years is home improvement. Yes, having a handy mate who is not afraid to get dirty can benefit both men and women. Men love the idea of having a little assistance in maintaining the home, even if it's just you showing interest or holding a flashlight.

Keep in mind that we are working to make ourselves available to full-grown men, not a man-child who will be intimidated by strong, smart, and sexy women. Do you really have time for those who still haven't figured out that women are complete human beings and gender roles can hinder the things we are naturally good at? I'm not

34

saying I don't believe that a man should open the car door for a woman or that he should not take out the trash, depending on the situation. Those are absolute requirements for "me" in a relationship. But in every relationship, we have to choose what works best for us.

For example, if your mate works midnights and you are home all day, will you wait until he comes in from work in the morning to take the trash out because it's man's work? Or, are you going to make sure the trash is out that night, in case the garbage man gets to you before he arrives, or just out of courtesy because he probably will return dead-ass tired? Sis, I hope you would just take the damn trash out. Being an asset, and not a liability, includes making life easier for the other person, not harder.

The more we know and the more that we can do in partnership, will ultimately make us more valuable to ourselves and to those we choose to spend our private time with. We raise our net worth by learning as much as possible, which inevitably makes us a great catch! The goal is to know how to do many things, not to always try to do everything ourselves. If your man is the best cook in the relationship, then let him be the cook, and you can handle cleaning up, or if you like cooking as well, take turns cooking and cleaning, or do it together.

Finding and choosing a mate is about two people coming together to make each other's lives more enjoyable and easier. If we could do everything ourselves, what would we need a mate for? Every relationship requires balance, and everyone desires to be loved, wanted, and appreciated. I can do a lot of things for myself and by myself, but I **LOVE** and appreciate when I meet the right person who can do those things for me or with me.

Chapter 3

Dating Safely in the New Millennium

Beware of the Bitter Man!

Did you know that there is actually a scientific explanation for that feeling you get when something is off? Have you ever met or talked to someone and there was something about them that you just did not like? Did you disregard that feeling because he was handsome, educated, a "catch," or you thought you were just being paranoid? Did you realize later that you should have followed your first mind? Now more than ever, we must move, first and foremost, using our instincts as a guide. The veil is thin, and our ancestors are talking to us.

Never underestimate your own internal alarm when it tells you that something is off. With the advent of the internet and social media, we are often subjected to this virtual reality that looks very different from what we experience when we leave our homes. With this in mind, we must acknowledge that not everyone operates from a place of love, respect, and good character, so proceed with caution.

Because of our ever-challenging, busy lives, it may be hard to notice right away if the dude you are dealing with is bitter. If you see that he is succumbing to this modern-day attempt to annihilate and attack womanhood, then he may be angry. These men, aka suspects, can often be found whining on (or discussing) a podcast about Black women, specifically, not being submissive or that Black women won't let them lead. So, in all fairness, let's take a moment of our time to give them the attention that far too many of them are undoubtedly crying for. Hmmm, OK, enough of that!

Beware because those are the types of males you want to avoid and not even bother engaging in conversations with. It is a complete waste of energy to try and sway him. There are far too many men in the world who are not so easily swayed by attention-seekers online for you to waste your time on the ones who are. In case you are wondering, as I am, how exactly did we get here? Some say it may have started with the disrespect toward women in music, and most likely has evolved from there. In retrospect, no one can pinpoint exactly when, but everyone agrees that we must change how we do things, especially how we treat and speak to each other. 2-Pac said it first!

It must be acknowledged that this modern display of hyper-male misogyny can be dangerous, which is why we must remain vigilant and aware of it. Often, the offenders start with small offenses (such as insults) that continue to grow as they become more comfortable with the woman. Dating a closet misogynist can be a threat to your mental and physical health, livelihood, and life.

Here is a compiled list of some of the suggested Dos and Don'ts when dating various male personality types, which sometimes fall into the Danger Zone. Since most men who grew up in the United States are likely to be misogynistic to some degree, we have to be aware and resistant to the sense of entitlement that often comes along with it. Keep in mind that this is a lighthearted, comedic guide, and there are exceptions to the rules. First and foremost, always use your own judgment and follow your instincts!

Archetype / Safety Guidelines

Type Of Men	His Story	Do	Don't	Outcome/Reasons
The Hobo-Sexual. Couch Surfer	Lives with an ex or cousin. Does not own anything but his flashy clothes. Has a newer car that he cannot afford. Is great in bed. In between jobs.	Only extremely protected sex if you are determined to.	Move him into your home. Fall for him. Accept gifts if you are not serious about him. Allow him to leave anything overnight.	It will be hard to get rid of him. He values appearances over security. Bad investment. May try and impregnate you for security. DANGER.

Type Of Men	His Story	Do	Don't	Outcome/Reasons
The Hobo-Sexual. Couch Surfer **Continued**	Looking for a 50/50 situation. Cleans up after himself when he visits; he learned early on that's how to get in. Has children already, maybe by numerous women.			
The Spontaneous Guy Manipulator Workaholic (Over 40)	Calls you on the day of wanting to go out because he is so busy. Translation: he wants to put you on his schedule, so it is convenient for him. Financially secure, most likely tired all the time. Will take you to nice places when he can, which will not be often. May have two or fewer children with the same woman.	Make him plan dates in advance, three days minimum. Keep him at arm's length. Put his ass on a schedule.	Sleep with him too soon unless you don't plan on keeping him around. Stop seeing other men until it's official. Underestimate him; he's sneaky….	Has a rotation of willing participants. He is overly confident and requires discipline. May have potential. Sex may be whack due to no stamina.

Dating Safely in the New Millennium

Type Of Men	His Story	Do	Don't	Outcome/Reasons
The Cub (Under 34, for women who are cougars)	More than a decade younger. Loves to date older women. Eager to please in bed. Works, but money is tight. Plans on being a millionaire by 40. Thinks all women are beautiful flowers and he's just a busy bee. Hang on to your every word. Still smells like he has breast milk in his mouth. Penis looks practically new.	Handle with care. Have protected sex. Have fun. Make him pay for the majority of things.	Take him too seriously. Get attached. Coddle him. Fall for him. Stay too long. Stop seeking potential long-term mates or use your best moves in bed. DO NOT PLAY WITH HIS EMOTIONS.	He does not know himself. It's not real. The sex is intoxicating. May look at you as a mother figure. Use your best moves and you may end up with a brick in your window, or worse, when he is cut off. DANGER.
The Aspiring Polygamist, (aka Jack and the Beanstalk Manipulative Narcissistic Charismatic	Extremely suave and convincing. No real income. Most likely hung like a horse. Preaches of Black unity and family, but he is always struggling or hustling. Blames all of his problems on the white man. Uses his place in the community to oppress the	Run for the border unless this dude is RICH and can afford multiple women. Afford means ALL of your needs AND wants are met,then you can discuss. Accept all the gifts.	Engage with him. Don't take him seriously. Don't birth his babies. Don't buy his magical beans and dreams of liberation from the couch. Do not limit yourself to his semi-hard, overused penis and potential STI's.	You will most likely grow out of this belief system as you mature. You may be left with a child or children, and child support will be minuscule, if any. He is passively controlling. He may become dangerous if he can no longer manipulate and control you.

Type Of Men	His Story	Do	Don't	Outcome/Reasons
The Aspiring Polygamist, (aka Jack and the Beanstalk Manipulative Narcissistic Charismatic- **Continued**	women in his life while he sows his oats. Thinks he deserves more than one woman, although he lacks in many areas. Has a short temper but appears peaceful.			
Community Penis (sometimes known as The Catch)	Has slept with numerous women in the community that you know of. Imagine the ones you do not know of. Looking for the perfect woman to settle down and have kids with. Financially secure or close to it.	Extremely protected sex. Keep him at arm's length. Expect disappointments.	Tell anyone you know you are dating him until you are at the altar. Be too available. Expect much more than disappointments.	You will find out you ain't the only one and forever be surrounded by a sea of exes unless you leave the city. He most likely will cheat in the future.

Dating Safely in the New Millennium

Type Of Men	His Story	Do	Don't	Outcome/Reasons
Union Worker-includes: Factory Worker Postal Worker Casino Worker	Works 60- hour weeks on the factory line. Drives a new employee-discounted car. Has rental property in the city that he is always working on. Indebted to child support. Waiting for retirement and that is all he will ever talk about.	Use your discretion. Understand he probably has a work wife. Accept all the gifts.	Expect too much stamina. Be surprised if you have to jump-start the penis.	These men's bodies are usually broken down by the time they are 45, depending on when they start working at these jobs. They are always grouchy and tired.
The Good Guy/Sneaky Smiling Bastard	Tell you he is a good guy. He is not. Has all of his shit together, so why is he single? Serial dater and finds fault in every woman. Has too many options.	Take your time to get to know him. Maintain your own autonomy.	Believe every word he says. Let your guard down too soon. Let him change who you are to fit his image.	These are harder to decode because they seem harmless, and each is different but has the same agenda, just for dating.

43

Pimpette Chronicles

Type Of Men	His Story	Do	Don't	Outcome/Reasons
Aging in the "closet".	Is Homophobic. Wants to live out his older years in a traditional relationship. Will never admit his sexuality, and if you find out, don't tell him you know. Ever!	Practice safe sex.	Ask him about his sexuality more than once. Dismiss him based on suspicion.	You will find out eventually. COULD BE DANGEREROUS IF HE IS IN THE CLOSET AND YOU FIND OUT.
The Dreamer/ Creative/ Musician	Always creating something. In tune with nature. Changes his mind like the weather. Always trying to figure out life. Has extreme quiet spells where he must be left alone. Will have you collecting rocks and howling at the moon. Most likely hung like a horse.	Practice safe sex.	Practice safe sex.	Who knows, he is still creating it, and you are a willing participant.

Dating Safely in the New Millennium

Type Of Men	His Story	Do	Don't	Outcome/Reasons
The Video Game Dude	Addicted to video Games. Will spend more time with his homies, or online, than with you. Is overweight or soon to be. May not hold a steady job, but if he does, the order of importance will be game, job, then you.	If you like taking care of a man-child and don't want to worry about cheating, he's your man! Practice safe sex.	Expect him to lead you anywhere other than GameStop. Practice safe sex, although he probably has no time to cheat.	Life will be mundane but most likely stable. He is the least likely to cheat because who the fuck wants him?
The Sugar Daddy	Usually, ten more years your senior. Has an excess of disposable cash. Does not mind paying for everything. He won't think he is your man. Looking for more companionship than anything.	Practice extreme safe sex. The older they are, the more likely to have been exposed to STIs. Know you can be replaced easily.	Settle for less than you know you deserve but be reasonable. Stop enjoying life with friends or seeking potential, permanent partners.	Could last for years. If he falls in love with you and it is beneficial to you in the long term, it can lead to marriage. Sex may not be great but depends on how well he has taken care of himself and whether or not he is willing to take the little blue pill.

45

Now that we have identified "some" of the archetypes of men you may encounter along your journey and their not-so-likable characteristics here is an example situation:

The Hobo-Sexual

Samania was a college student working full-time at a local call center. She'd recently moved into a nice apartment and was excited to have a space all to herself. She had been dating a man named Raj for a few months but had never been over to his place. They met on campus, where he told her he was a student. In the beginning, it was exciting when he'd sneak into her dorm room and spend the night. With the freedom of her own apartment, she could only dream of the fun they would have when he visited.

As time progressed and she grew comfortable in her new home, she began to notice that he was always there and, slowly but surely, had started leaving his personal items around. One day it was a toothbrush, the next, his entire game system. At first, she did not mind, but then she started to see that he never went to his classes and that he was never at the job he claimed to have had. Eventually, Raj told her he'd been kicked out of school for having illegal drugs on him and recently lost his job.

Samania felt sorry for him, so she allowed him to stay. But soon, he began to feel more like a burden and less like fun. She would come home to him playing video games in his drawers while her home would be a mess. On top of that, she learned she was pregnant. Raj begged her to keep the baby and promised that he would help more around the house and work harder to find a job. That lasted for about a month, and then the verbal abuse began. Raj was always angry and would often yell and scream at her. He would sometimes tell her she was fat and ugly and that no one else would want her now that she was pregnant with a baby. He was now so brave that he admitted he purposely impregnated her because he owned her.

Soon she learned that he had been kicked out of college years ago and had been staying on campus with friends. On top of that, he had a reputation as a couch surfer. The entire relationship was set up from the beginning. Samania had been trapped and Raj was just looking for a woman to support him and provide a roof over his head all along.

Now some of you may be thinking, why would someone want to impregnate a woman they probably don't want to be with, just for a place to live? In the larger picture, Raj will eventually have to pay or owe Samania child support until that child reaches 18 at the minimum. Well, quite frankly, when you are homeless, you can only address the immediate challenge at hand, which, in this case, was shelter.

People in life and death situations will often do things they normally may not do just to survive. Keep in mind that the current unemployment rate, coupled with the growing number of male homeless in the United States, has led to an influx of hobo-sexuals in our communities. These men do not look like your everyday homeless person and may even have a job and a car. Still, their focus is securing shelter, so they date with the intent of swooning a woman long enough to move into her home. They are often men who, starting from a young age, moved in with girlfriends and then were kicked out once the relationship went sour.

Because of this cyclical behavior, they are forced to leave everything they may have built with that partner and start over time and time again. It is a cycle that they do not know how to get out of. In many inner-cities and BIPOC communities, it is common practice for men to move in with women. They are never completely the head of the household, and the woman knows it. The power dynamics are severely unbalanced from the start of these types of relationships. This often leads to conflict, and when arguments occur, some women won't hesitate to remind the man that he lives in her home.

Once these lines are crossed, even when they reconcile, the man will always hold a little resentment toward the woman for having his manhood and ability to lead the relationship attacked. For this and many other reasons, I strongly suggest you use extreme caution when moving a man into your home or moving into his. If you decide to cohabitate with someone who is not your husband, please consider seeking a new place that you both can move into together.

Building a home together is much easier than making space for someone in your home. Even those with the best intentions will cringe when someone is in our space moving things around. Creating a space together sets the basis for a more balanced relationship and environment. It also reinforces teamwork as you work together to make it your home.

Dating Safely and Ethically

As a '70s baby growing up in the '80s, I was often reminded of a simple rule that, in actuality, could end most of the world's problems if everyone committed to following it. The words my granny would tell me were simply, "Treat people the way you want to be treated." Being able to put yourself in someone else's shoes and see things from their perspective has always helped keep me on the right path.

During my dating journey, I continue to aspire to be as honest and open with my partner as possible. Sometimes even too honest, I have been told. Surprisingly, some people simply do not want the truth, but that's a story for another day. As for now, I would like to share some of the rules I have utilized that have kept me safe along the way.

- Do not assume every man is mentally stable. Some of our biggest serial killers have been what folks call "the nice guy." Those nice men often appear so nice because they hide some serious issues. Take your time to get to know him and see how he responds to stressful situations before you completely trust him.

- On those first few dates, do not leave your drink unattended. Too many women are getting slipped date rape drugs, and it ain't nothing new. Again, don't assume everyone operates from a place of love and respect. Predators are usually the ones you least expect and often the ones everyone else will tend to protect and support.

- Always let someone you trust know where you are going and who you will be with. I have been known to even send a picture of the person. I don't care if you are 25 or 65; someone needs to be aware of who you are with.

- If meeting for the first time, meet in a public, well-populated place, and make sure you mention that someone knows who you are meeting. I will even throw in the fact that I sent them a picture of my date.

- Do not play games with his emotions. No matter what, never pretend to care about anyone just to get something out of them. This can be deadly. This goes back to treating people the way you want to be treated. Simple.

- Do not accept expensive gifts from him if you know you do not want to be with him. Some men will give out of the kindness of their hearts, while others give to assert some sort of dominance and control over you. Those are the ones who are quick to demand something they gave you back once the relationship goes sour. My best practice is, if ever it goes sour and I am unsure how he feels, I will offer to give an expensive gift back. Most men will not want it, but just in case.

- Early in the courtship, refrain from accepting expensive gifts altogether unless, again, you are certain this will be your mate.

- If he asks for a gift back, give it to him if you can. You can always replace a material item. You, on the other hand, can never be replaced.

- Do not take him to your home until you are sure he will be around for a while. This one is tricky because, in actuality, there have been cases where victims have been dating for months, and once they break it off, the man still becomes violent. This goes back to trusting your own instincts to determine whether he can become a threat or not, but again do not underestimate.

- While your children are young, you date first and foremost with them in mind. That means considering the potential mate and what he will bring to you and your family as a whole. What type of parent is he if he has kids? What is his relationship like with his own family? Also, remember, blended families are tough, but that's an entire book in itself.

- Do not bring him around your children until you are close or sure it will be a committed relationship. At that point, you observe how he acts around your children and how he engages with them. Does he seem uninterested? Does he seem agitated? Does he seem patient? Do his actions seem fake or forced?

- Do not leave your children with your boyfriend. Too many times, we see mothers grieving because they left their children with their boyfriends. Sadly, some men simply are unable to love other men's children, and some will even develop hatred toward them because they are getting your attention where he could be.

- If you ever see signs that a man does not "like" your child, simply move on.

- If you are on a date or in a situation, and it becomes hostile, don't argue with a fool or person you don't really know. Remain calm and try to diffuse the situation. You don't have to have the last word. You do not need to bring him down a peg. Let him be the one who is out of line if it gets to that point. Once you are safe, never speak to him again.

- When you decide to have sex, make sure you see him put that condom on correctly and inspect that dick. I always say if you are woman enough to have sex, then be woman enough to look at the penis. Flip it over and examine it every time until you are in a committed relationship and you trust him. If something seems strange, ask a question, and if it doesn't seem right, now is the time to have a headache.

- Do not loan him money, and try not to let him use your car for any reason. If you must with the car situation, make sure he has the money to replace your vehicle if something happens, and you are certain that he will. Use your own discretion with both and ask yourself, is it appropriate that he even asked you? Just how well and how long have you known him again?

- In the beginning stages, do not leave money or jewelry lying around your house while he is over. I cannot believe how many women get *got* by some of the men they let into their homes. I've even heard of a dude stealing one girl's jewelry and giving it to another chick. The audacity!

Now that we have gone over some very general rules to follow, it would be remiss if we were not to touch on violence in relationships. As mentioned previously, this guide will mostly focus on the dating process since dating often leads to courtship, and courtship may lead to a relationship. We will examine these three stages in a subsequent chapter, but for now, let's explore other ways to remain vigilant.

Intimate Partner Violence

According to the National Coalition Against Domestic Violence[1], 1 in 4 women will experience sexual violence, physical violence, or stalking by an intimate partner during their lifetime. Over 43 million women in the United States have experienced psychological aggression from a partner in their lifetime. There are four types of IPV, which the CDC has described as Intimate Partner Violence behaviors:

1. **Physical violence:** when a person hurts or tries to hurt a partner by hitting, kicking, or using another type of physical force.

2. **Stalking:** a pattern of repeated, unwanted attention and contact by a partner that causes fear or concern for one's own safety or the safety of someone close to the victim.

3. **Sexual violence:** forcing or attempting to force a partner to take part in a sex act, sexual touching, or a non-physical

---

[1] National Coalition Against Domestic Violence
https://www.cdc.gov/violenceprevention/intimatepartnerviolence/fastfact.html

sexual event (e.g., sexting) when the partner does not or cannot consent. For example, you are passed out drunk, and the person has sex with you anyway.

4. **Psychological aggression:** the use of verbal and non-verbal communication with the intent to harm another partner mentally or emotionally and/or to exert control over another partner.

With numbers as high as 1 in 4, you are considered an anomaly if you manage to get through life without experiencing some sort of abuse. As a woman, we must always be looking to protect our mental and physical health and our exterior beauty. When someone meets you, the first thing they notice is your exterior. While we would like to pretend that looks don't matter, they absolutely do.

Being in a relationship where physical abuse is present could ultimately damage your ability to attract future mates once you are out of that relationship. This in no way implies that it is impossible, but it will most likely become harder. Women who find themselves in these relationships can be left toothless, eyeless, with hearing loss, or any other deformities or issues they did not have coming into the relationship. Some "males" will intentionally disfigure you in hopes of leaving you less appealing to future potential mates. It's a sad, harsh truth. Physical and mental abuse can completely destroy your self-esteem and affect your attractiveness. Women who are abused must work hard to regain self-confidence and seek counseling.

As mentioned previously, every woman has something beautiful about her, and the glow of a well-loved and taken care of woman always shines through. When we are in situations where we are made to feel unloved and suffer from any type of abuse, it will inevitably age us inside and out. Heartache and pain can be shown whether there are physical scars or not. Notice how beautifully the well-loved wife ages, as opposed to the wife who has experienced countless disappointments and heartbreaks? We will all experience pain in our lifetime, but the key is to really know when to walk away from a bad situation.

There may be times when you have to pull up your big girl panties and say enough is enough. Sometimes you may even need to cry yourself to sleep after a breakup but know when to stop crying. Granted, there is no appropriate time limit for grieving; keep in mind that crying all the time can take years off your looks and life. One of the most powerful skills one can learn is how to control their own thoughts. Our thoughts are why some of us cannot move forward, but they can also be the reason we do.

If you can learn how to control your thoughts, you will become one powerful Bitch! Sometimes it will require you to take time to heal by staying away from people for a while. Or it may be as simple an act as not listening to songs that bring back memories. Whatever triggers the pain while trying to heal, immediately remove yourself from it in whatever way you need. By taking care of yourself, protecting yourself (including your thoughts), and being kind to yourself, you are ensuring that you are the **"best version of you"** and that you are moving in **POWER!**

Getting To Know Him

It's always exciting to meet someone new and begin to build a connection. When you are getting to know a potential mate, remember that they are always going to first introduce you to their representative. This is the person that they want the world to see them as and not completely who they are. This being will show you all the good in him, his absolute best qualities. Most believe that it usually takes at least three months for that person to let their guard down and start sharing the not-so-great parts about them. I believe it to be six months in these modern times. Pay close attention during this stage to get an idea of who you are really dealing with.

First, I want you to learn exactly what type of social life he already has. What does he do for fun, and who does he spend his time with? Depending on the age and status of the potential mate, he may have friends he spends a lot of time with or friends he seldom sees. If he is dedicated to upward mobility, it will be apparent. I have learned that men who are focused on building a legacy or making money tend to surround themselves with people who either have it or are on the same mission. Are you familiar with the saying, birds of a feather flock together? This is true in all aspects of life.

If you start to notice that he and his friends are sitting around cursing, drinking, and high all of the time, it is likely that is what he will continue to do. If his friends always have a new girl around, take note of that, too. That does not mean your fella is the same, but just observe how your dude responds to these women and situations. Does he seem to think this behavior is good or bad, or is he indifferent?

If the men discuss investments or ways to make money, then that will most likely always be his main focus. If he is community-oriented, that will be what drives him as well. Remember, the type of man you choose is a direct reflection of you, and during the relationship, you are destined to take on some of his traits and vice versa.

Now is it possible to meet a man, depending on his age, and introduce him to new things that may steer him away from his friends if they are the go-nowhere and do-nothing types? Absolutely, but for how long? Most of us over 30 will start to analyze our circle and the people we spend our time with. It's OK to hang out and kick it with friends at any age, but just be sure that the man you choose is serious-minded and about his business first and foremost. Your goal should always be to surround yourself with people who are doing positive things in their lives.

Another very important thing I take note of when getting to know a potential mate, is his relationship with the women in his world. This includes his mother, sisters, daughters, etc. You can learn a lot about a man by how he treats his mother. A man who has no respect for his mom will most likely not have any respect for you. This does not necessarily mean to exclude men who were not raised by their mother for whatever reason; this means to be mindful of the reasons and how he speaks to and relates to her.

On the other hand, also be wary of men who are in emotionally incestual relationships with their mothers. These men tend to seek approval from their mommies and will often reference their mom as a role model or prototype for what they want their woman to be like. He may even say childish things like, "My momma will always come first," or "Ain't nobody more important than Momma," etc. At that moment, you need to decide if you want to compete with his mommy for the rest of your life.

As an emotionally balanced woman, you will understand that you would never put your man in a position where he has to choose between his mother/daughter/sister or you, so hearing such ridiculous comments from a grown ass man lets you know that you and him ain't even on the same wavelength. Your man should be wise enough not to pit you against the other women in his life and that those relationships are to be honored and respected alongside, yet separately from his relationship with you. Never should you feel you are in competition, and if you start to feel that way, step back and let her have him.

The second relationship you should be observant of is his relationship with the mother of his children. Does he speak badly about her or talk down on her? Does he constantly complain about her? Is he even in his children's life? How often does he see them? These questions will give you enormous insight into this man's character. If he is the type to say nasty things about the mother of his children, do not engage or encourage it. We understand that not all relationships end well, and there may have been very specific reasons why they ended that you may not need to know right away. But regardless, a man with any amount of good character will be reluctant to speak ill of his children's mother. If he needs to discuss the issues he has with the mother of his children, encourage him to do so with a counselor or the minister of his church. That definitely should not be your role in his life. Remember, there are always two sides to every story; if she is an issue, you will learn in due time. But for now, while you are getting to know him, discourage the baby momma drama by not engaging. If he brings it up, simply change the subject. You are not his therapist. As time progresses, you will learn all you need to know, and once you are a family, it will be appropriate to discuss the ex to an extent but still discourage disrespect.

Additionally, please pay close attention to how he responds to stress or expresses his anger. Is he constantly beefing with someone? Does he have road rage? Is he rude to the wait staff or other people in front of you? Does he appear to want to be dominant over others?

Is he calm one moment and flying off the handle the next? Does he exhibit hypermasculinity-type behaviors? Is he homophobic or misogynistic?

Remember, when men are not secure with their masculinity, they will always look for ways to assert dominance and prove that they are "manly." These types of men are usually loud, obnoxious, attention-seeking, and weak. They are quick to dismiss you and do not value perspectives that empower or uplift women. If they come across a social media post pointing out a common male flaw, they will immediately point out a female one, as if it somehow erases the previous one. Some of these men will even go as far as to describe themselves as the notorious **"alpha male."**

Just know if a man has to call himself an **"alpha,"** then he definitely ain't one. These fellas generally make the worst type of mate. When they fail at home, work, school, etc., they will look for someone to dominate and blame. In relationships, it will always be their woman. After all, if you have little or no control over the other aspects of your life, what easier way to seek validation than to assert yourself over the woman who loves you?

Lastly, let's talk some more about abusive relationships. As mentioned previously, 1 in 4 women will find themselves experiencing some form of abuse, so let's also note that homicide is the second leading cause of death of Black females aged 1-19, and for

Black women aged 20-44, it is the 4th in the U.S. It is a sad fact that the majority of the victims fall prey to someone who claimed to have loved them.

While most of us know that if he hits you once, he will hit you again, let's also acknowledge that any form of abuse damages you as a whole. Verbal abuse, aka emotional abuse, can leave you broken and questioning your self-worth, though it is often harder to know that you are being abused. Verbally abusive men are often hyper-critical and will make you feel like you can't do anything right. He will insult you out of the blue and pretend that he is just joking, and if you bring it to his attention, he will say that you are being sensitive or overreacting.

Abusers often ignore boundaries, invade your privacy, are possessive and controlling, and are dismissive of your feelings. These types of men have an ultimate goal: to manipulate, intimidate, and gain power over you. Any emotionally mature man will not desire to control another human being. Be wary of anyone who tries to assert dominance in your life in any regard.

Protecting Yourself!

In my lifetime, I have gotten to know many types of people, including dope men, scholars, pimps, hoes, politicians, preachers, and so on.

Dating Safely in the New Millennium

What I have learned is that everything is not always as it seems, and people often have a masterful way of hiding their true selves.

I have found those who lacked what some would consider "good character," were sometimes those whom society may deem the most trusting. Often our biggest threat comes from the ones who appear to be harmless or the ones that others hold in the highest esteem. Is it uncommon to hear of the preacher being caught molesting the children at the church or the police officer killing his wife? Since, often, folks who mean us no good have spent a lifetime hiding their true selves, what should you do if you meet or end up with Mr. Hyde?

The fact that 72% of murder-suicides involve an intimate partner, and 94% of these victims are women, according to NCADV[2], sheds light on just how important prevention is when it comes to protecting yourself. When taking a closer look at intimate partner homicides, 20% of those victims were not even the partners, but family members, friends, neighbors, persons who intervened, law enforcement responders, or bystanders. That means that the type of people we bring into our lives could not only be a threat to ourselves but also to those around us. When analyzing this problem as a whole, I believe that avoiding those who are more likely to cause issues later down the line is our best defense from becoming one of these statistics.

---

[2] National Coalition Against Domestic Violence
https://ncadv.org/statistics

It has been said that men take rejection a lot worse than women, and many men will openly admit that they cannot handle half of the pain, that they often willingly and carelessly dish out to the women in their lives. If a man commits adultery, he is likely forgiven, but even in this so-called modern day and age, women are ostracized and villainized, as in the case of Jada P. and Will. Men and women often cannot fathom the thought of a woman doing what men have done for centuries.

Just think how there have been numerous songs for decades that openly suggest murder as a suitable punishment for a woman stepping out on her man, but if the song was about a man who had been caught cheating, the song would most likely suggest forgiveness and redemption. It is no secret that violence is literally embedded in the fabric of this patriarchal society we call America, so it should not be surprising how little women are valued, protected, and respected, especially Black women. With this knowledge, it is not only our duty, but our right to protect ourselves.

Often, we hear stories and wonder why the victim did not leave earlier, why no one intervened, or how they missed those notorious red flags we love to talk about. But like most situations in life, sometimes you don't know who you are dealing with until it is too late. Too many times, we blame the victim, but we rarely take a close look at the society that makes it far too easy for many of us to become victimized. I personally am not one to operate from a place of victimhood, and I believe in empowerment in all situations.

Most of us consider ourselves good judges of character, but one must also acknowledge that you can never put anything past anyone. So, the question remains, how do you prevent getting into a situation that may not be so easy to get out of? My answer is to always have an **exit strategy.** This should actually begin the moment you start dating someone.

Naively, many of us dream of what type of life we would have with that person or what kind of wedding we will throw. Instead of all the fairytales, I have found it even more useful to develop and start thinking of ways to get rid of the dude if the relationship goes sour or if he becomes a threat. Some of the men we come across in life may require an exit plan as simple as telling him you are no longer interested and maybe blocking the number. But in extreme cases, you may have to move your residence completely.

I know the latter may seem crazy, but if death by homicide was not the second and fourth leading cause of death for Black females, with most perpetrators likely to have been someone who was supposed to love them, this subject would not need to be addressed. Jaded lovers have too often become many of our realities, and it matters little what level of life experience, education, or economic status you are in.

Not All Fairytales Come True

Cynthia was a beautiful 58-year-old mother of two college-aged students when she ran into her crush from high school, Leon. He was as handsome and smooth as she remembered him being so many years ago. Cynthia, now a registered nurse, had done very well for herself in her life. She had a beautiful home in the suburbs and owned several nice vintage sports cars. After going through a divorce and dealing with her now-ex-husband's infidelity, she was ready to get back to dating.

In high school, as an awkward teen, she never had a chance to get to know Leon. Now so many decades later, it felt like destiny. Their first conversation flowed so effortlessly, and he made her feel like she was a teen again. He told her that he worked at a factory and that he, too, had just divorced. He would soon reveal that he was paying a shipload of child support for his four children (that his wife was keeping from him), and he had to downsize to a small apartment downtown. He said the divorce had destroyed him financially, but he would be back on top in no time. Being financially secure, Cynthia didn't care about his economic status and said she didn't need a man for his money and was more than capable of taking care of herself.

As the months passed, Leon would bring her roses, and they would go on walks by the riverwalk holding hands. He began claiming her as his girlfriend, and Cynthia was honored to have caught the attention of someone who was once one of the most popular guys in high school. After just six months of dating, he asked her to marry him, and she accepted. She felt lucky to have nabbed this sweet romantic guy so soon after divorcing. They went to Vegas and eloped before her children had even met him. They were both getting older, so there was no need for delay, they said upon their return.

Leon moved into Cynthia's house, and immediately things changed. The first thing he did was sell off her sports cars because he felt they were a waste of money since she rarely drove them. Next, he put her kids' belongings in storage in the basement because he said they rarely visited, so why should they have an entire bedroom to themselves? Having grown up with the notion of the man leading the house, Cynthia agreed with his decision. Her children came home to learn that they no longer had their own space and immediately did not like Leon. They told their mother that something was off about him.

On weekends, Leon insisted on taking Cynthia with him to the casino to reassure her that he was not a cheater like her ex, but after she started complaining about the amount of time he spent there, he would just go alone. Sometimes he would come home angry and reeking alcohol, and that's when the arguing would start. As time went on, she would soon learn that his marriage ended because he had a gambling problem, and she would also learn that the money he received from her cars he blew at the casino instead of putting it in a joint account like he said. Then the physical abuse started. It began with just a smack he swore would never happen again, but then it progressed to him once choking her until she was unconscious. She awoke to him holding her and crying. He begged her not to leave him like everyone else in his life had done. She said only if he went to get help. He agreed.

Leon promised never to hurt her again and agreed to attend domestic abuse prevention classes. Eventually, he stopped going, and again, the abuse started. One day, she went to work, and a co-worker noticed a bruise on her arm. That's when Cynthia broke down and confessed. She said she was embarrassed that she was almost 60 years old and getting beat by her husband. In all the 30-plus years of her first marriage, she said that her first husband had never laid a hand on her. Had she known that physical abuse was the alternative to a cheating spouse, she would have stayed with the cheater.

In tears, Cynthia cried that she could not believe she had gotten herself into this, especially so late in life. The co-worker told her how she, too, had experienced abuse and urged her to leave. She wanted to make Cynthia realize how bad her situation could become, but Cynthia did not see it. Cynthia said she was not going to leave everything she worked so hard for behind and that he was the one who would have to go. She begged her co-worker never to tell a soul.

One day, Cynthia and Leon got into another argument, but we will never know what it was about because this time Leon did not hit or choke Cynthia; instead, he pulled out a 5mm Glock, chased her out of the house, and murdered her on her front lawn. He then turned the gun on himself and blew his brains out.

Because Leon had nothing to lose, he had no problem taking everything away from Cynthia, including her life. It's easy for us to sit back and judge, say she ignored the red flags, say she should have just left, say all the things we think we would do if ever in this situation. But in no way could any of us say that Cynthia wanted her children to one day have to bury their mother.

Exit Strategy

When you first meet a man, I want you to find out exactly what he has to lose. Men who already have a good or decent life are not quick to throw it away due to a failed relationship. Most men who are happy with themselves know they can always get another woman. After all, the woman-to-man ratio is in their favor.

Some of the things that I take note of when evaluating a potential mate are:

- Does he have family members that he is close to?

- Does he have children, or a child, that he is close to, loves, and speaks of, and frequently?

- Does he like or love his job?

- Does he seem happy with himself, proud, confident, etc.?

- Is he financially secure? Not necessarily rich, but not broke?

- Does he seem sad, anxious, or depressed at all?

- Does he own nice things that he is proud of? A house, a nice car, etc.?

- What type of life has he lived thus far? Has he been to prison, homeless, abused, etc.?

- If he has been to prison, does he speak of what he learned or how horrible his experience was? Has he grown from this experience?

- Does he seem like he has low self-esteem? Walks with his head down, seems uninterested, criticizes himself, is insecure, etc.?

- Is he dealing with hardships in his life? On probation, DUI issues, financial issues, child support, baby momma problems, job stressors, health issues, any serious issues?

Men who are not in a great place in life should refrain from dating, but too many are looking for a way to feel better about themselves and choose women as a way of doing so. A long-standing practice has always been to "date" any woman simply for his own gratification. When dating, it is wise to wonder what his objective is while still being certain of your own. Unfortunately, we cannot expect unhealed men to heal themselves before coming at us, so we have to try and dodge them like the plague. It is not your job to fix a man upon arrival. Repeat after me, it is not your job to fix a man upon arrival.

To ensure that you are never looked at as an easy target or potential victim, there are plenty of things that you can do or say to make him think twice before stepping toward you. Here are some of my favorites:

1. Make it no secret that you have men in your life who love and care about you. Even if you are not close to your brothers, uncles, cousins, etc., he does not need to know that. Let it be known that you have a crazy cousin (even if you don't) or that you have a nephew on the police force. If you can, have him meet some of them as early as possible, if they won't embarrass you, of course.

2. Take self-defense classes, martial arts, kickboxing, etc., and speak of what you learned with excitement. Some men are intimidated by strong women, and some are turned on by them. For our purposes, we do not want the ones who are easily intimidated.

3. Get your CPL or CCW and let him know you are licensed to kill. You don't have to come off as GI Jane, but let a dude know you have no problem busting a cap in that ass if need be. A lot of men nowadays have theirs as well, so he should not be worried at all and will most likely see you as an asset. I don't need to remind you that if you have small children, never leave your gun where they can get it, and make sure you are properly trained and practice shooting often. Never pull out your gun unless you are certain you need to use it.

4. In the beginning, if you live alone, lead him to believe that you have a roommate who lives with you or a friend or relative who stays at your house sometimes, and do not let him know where you live until you are certain you want to keep him around, and you feel safe with him. Unfortunately, it is still very easy to find someone's address, so keep that in mind, too.

5. Always appear in control and never come off as a pushover. Men who are abusers try you in baby steps before it becomes full-on abuse. That play wrestling shit ain't always play wrestling, so know the difference. If you tell him to stop and he does not, take note. This is a red flag and shows that he doesn't understand boundaries.

6. If he does something you don't like, and you've told him, and he is dismissive, take that as a sign of things to come and move on.

Even with all the above in motion, you may still find yourself having to break off a relationship, or situationship, with someone who may not be so eager to let go. Don't choose violence first or even argue if you ever find yourself in this space. Strategically choose peace. This is when you put your well-thought-out exit strategy in place.

Example Exit Strategies

Situation	Strategy	Do not
He has invested large sums of money in you and given you some expensive gifts, but you want out. He is accusing you of using him. You are concerned for your safety. This dude seems off.	Tell him you just need some time to step back, offer to give him back his shit, go and stay at a friend's or family member's house that he does not know. Keep talking to him somewhat, but not too much, just enough to know where his mind is at. Gradually cut	- Argue with him, belittle him, or attack his character or manhood. - Meet him just to talk, meet him to give him his shit by yourself, completely cut off communication, talk shit, or tell him you ain't giving him back shit. - Show any weakness or

	off communication so that he can focus on some other chick. Drop his gifts (if he insists that you return them) off to someone you both know, or maybe the police station. Wean him off gradually.	fear.
You just started dating and you want out. He has given you a few tokens of appreciation. He seems angry.	Firmly tell him you aren't interested. Tell him you decided to work it out with your ex. Block his number, but if he knows where you live, lay low for a while and keep your eyes open.	- Argue with him. Explain shit to him. Communicate with him.
He has shown signs of abuse or has already put his hands on you. You are scared of him and know that he can become violent.	Secretly and carefully look for a place where he cannot find you. Have someone safely and cautiously move your belongings, preferably when there is no chance of him being around. Please let them know the situation	- Argue with him. - Beg him to leave you alone. - Show weakness or fear. - Hesitate to leave. - Ever go back once you are free

	and proceed with caution. Move out asap, and do not hesitate. Get a personal protection order, but only after you are sure he can't find you. It is literally a piece of paper that cannot protect you in reality, but if you are forced to defend yourself, it works in your favor. Truth is, there are plenty of dead women who had a ppo over their abusers.	

Remember, your exit strategy is unique to your situation and develops the more you get to know him. Once you know his temperament, you must use your wit and instincts to leave a relationship peacefully. Sometimes you may have to make the man break up with you just to spare his bruised ego. Whatever you need to do to get out, do it.

There are plenty of women in prison because they let domestic violence situations get out of control and end up taking the life of their abuser. Please know that the biased injustice system often shows no mercy to these women. Sadly, some women will unfortunately still end up dead. My question is, if it ever comes down to you or him, who will you choose?

Life With Marco - Trigger Warning, Abuse/Rape -

Adaoma was barely 16 years old when she met him. He was 11 years her senior and ran a small business. Marco had one child that was still in diapers, whom he adored more than anything. Adaoma's home life was filled with fighting, drinking, and chaos, so any opportunity to get away to find some peace was welcomed. Coming from a dysfunctional home himself, they shared stories of how their alcoholic mothers would beat them when they were angry. Sometimes their phone conversations would last until the morning, and they would fall asleep on the phone. Being a loner, she was happy to have found a friend she could talk to. Marco shared his dreams of someday marrying and having at least four more children.

One evening, Marco picked her up from school and took her to his house. He taught her how to smoke weed and introduced her to Bacardi 151. She felt like an adult as they listened to music and chilled. She had never smoked weed and had only sipped out of her parents' drinks on occasion. She had no idea what the combination of weed and alcohol would do to her. She passed out and awoke to Marco pulling her pants down.

Dating Safely in the New Millennium

Adaoma, who had only attempted sex once, lay in the bed paralyzed. She had no idea that he looked at her in a sexual way, and she thought of the chubby older man as a friend. Tears rolled down her face as he continued to pleasure himself while she lay there. He took no notice of her pain and, when it was over, actually handed her his shotgun to take a picture with. It was her own fault, she told herself. She had no business being over at his house and definitely not lying in his bed. She should have said something instead of just lying there. How stupid and naïve she had been.

One day, Adaoma and her mother got into a fight, and she ran away to Marco's house. He urged her to return home, but she said she could no longer live there. The abuse was getting worse, and her mother had bit her so hard that she had a huge bite mark on her arm. The beatings had evolved to the point where she had to start defending herself. She knew it was wrong, but it was hard to just lie and take a beating from a drunken woman who appeared to hate her, she said. Adaoma knew she could never win, but at least she could get her off of her if she at least tried.

Marco allowed her to live with him and she was happy to have been free. His house was nasty, and he owned a cat that peed everywhere, but at least it was quiet there, she thought. When she moved in, she cleaned everything, and made the place a home. She had always been very independent, so she knew how to cook and clean like Miss Celie from *The Color Purple*. She would eventually get used to the grotesque sex that came with him, and it was better than the chaos and misery at home.

In the beginning, Marcos would take her to and from school because he said he wanted her to continue her education. When she met him, she was failing most of her classes, but with Marcos showing an interest in her education, she was soon getting all As. At home, no one had stressed the importance of education, and her mother never tried to force her to go to school. Her mother was too concerned with the fights and drunken nights she would spend with her boyfriend to notice what was happening with her own children. Adaoma once said that her mother would get so drunk that she would totally destroy the house, and then, the next morning, her mother would wake her children up from their sleep by beating them with a broom, blaming them for the mess. Adaoma never slept a good night in her life.

When she showed Marco her first report card, instead of praise, he seemed disappointed. He thought she had gotten bad grades because she was stupid when it was because she hated to be around other teenagers, so she rarely went to class. Since education was not valued in her family, it was not a big deal. He then decided that she would be better off just taking a GED test, so she did.

At this point, she was happy to do anything he told her to do. Her life with Marco was the closest she had ever gotten to being at peace in her young life. When she lived at home, she was suicidal and severely depressed, and she often just stayed hiding in the closet away from all the noise. When she wasn't hiding, she spent most of her days caring for her younger siblings while attempting to go unnoticed. She never knew what would set her mother off.

One of the things that she loved about Marco was that he was so dedicated to being a father to his daughter. Her own father had moved out of state and left her behind. Adaoma's father would later reveal that he left the city because her mother was crazy and abusive to him. She remembered thinking that if he knew her mom was crazy, why in the hell did he leave his child behind and just start a new family?

Once out of school, her time was free to work alongside Marco and care for his daughter. Marco said Maria's mother had decided she did not want her and signed away her rights. Adaoma would later find out that he had bullied the mother to gain custody with threats. With Marco having full-time custody, Adaoma became his full-time babysitter. She was also responsible for tasks like typing contracts and making phone calls for his business. When his workers would not show up, she would help him move heavy equipment and carry ladders. The work was hard, and the days were long, but she eventually grew used to it all. He never paid her for any of her work but took care of her basic needs. He told her that was payment enough.

The years flew by, and Adaoma was now 19. Life with Marco was different but not necessarily better than her life at home had been. At least Marco never really physically hit her, just an occasional shake and smack every now and then, she said. She would always fight him back, but he was three times her size. Again, she could never win. Sometimes when he was angry, he would call her all kinds of sluts and bitches and tell her she wasn't shit. This only made her want to show him otherwise.

Let's not pretend that Adaoma was completely innocent, nor was every argument Marco's fault. But since she had grown up in a house where the parents argued all the time, she thought this behavior was normal and would call him fat bastards, bitches, punks, and her lowest blow was once telling him his mother was in hell sucking the devil's dick (Marco's mom was once a prostitute). Adaoma would come up with any insult she could muster to defend his verbal attacks. Growing up in the hood, she was well versed in playing the dozens. Often when they'd argue, he would threaten to send her back to her drunken mother, and he would tell her she would be nothing but a drunk someday, too. Because of this fear, Adaoma rarely drank alcohol, and she never took to smoking weed, either. She wanted to prove him wrong.

Adaoma did not have many friends, and Marco would insult and try to chase away the ones she did. He tried to control everything in her life, but although she was young, she still stood up to him. She was growing older, wiser, and tired of spending day in and day out battling with him. She eventually convinced Marco to teach her to drive, and he agreed. He took her on the road, deliberately made her nervous, and then yelled at her for making mistakes. He laughed and made her feel so incompetent.

What Adaoma really wanted more than anything was to just get married and have a family of her own. Marco told her she was too young and he was not sure she could take care of his children if something were to happen to him. Meanwhile, she was the primary caregiver for his daughter. He would often tell her that caring for Maria meant she was getting practice for their own children one day. He used the idea of marriage and a family as if it was some sort of carrot on a stick and string in front of an Ass. At that time in life, marriage was the most a girl like Adaoma, from a dysfunctional home, could hope for.

Time continued to pass, and Adaoma grew up. She would realize that she wanted more out of life, although she had no idea how to start. One day, one of her relatives called and asked her if she could go and stay with her cousin, who was away at college and needed someone to care for her new baby for a few months. Adaoma, eager to go anywhere, agreed. When Marco found out, he was unhappy, but he pretended he did not care. He even drove her to the bus stop to leave. She arrived safely in Ohio and was greeted by a crying baby that would now be her responsibility.

Seems like everywhere she went, she was expected to take care of someone else's children. With her cousin, she rarely even ventured outside of the home. At least with Marco, they often went to restaurants and the movies. Maybe life with him wasn't so bad after all.

One weekend, he talked her into letting him visit her and take her to a hotel. He chose a very nice one with a jacuzzi. She had never been to a nice hotel or on vacation in all her years. He told her that if she came back home, things would change. She agreed and left her cousin's home soon after. Immediately, Marco impregnated her with her first child, but still, he maintained that he did not want to marry. He said it was because they argued too much, and he did not want his kids growing up in a household like the one he and she experienced.

Adaoma was crushed to learn that she would have to have a child out of wedlock, like most women she knew. She had always envisioned her life differently.

Once the baby arrived, Marco sometimes held back on buying things for the baby as a form of punishment for Adaoma when she would not behave like he thought she should. Eventually, Adaoma grew tired of always being at his mercy, so she decided to start making money on her own. This way, she could buy what she wanted when she wanted to.

During the times she was searching for work, Marco offered to take her to job interviews, but each time he somehow managed to make her miss them. After a while, she stopped trusting him and learned how to catch the bus. When she returned, he would be angry but never said why. Soon, Adaoma was able to get a great job working at a hospital. They were so impressed by her test scores that they hired her on the spot. The job also had a daycare just across the street, so she didn't have to worry about childcare. When Marco learned of this, he was pissed! He told her that she would get fired within a week, and he had no idea how she managed to talk her way into such a great job. He was wrong.

Since he had already shown her that he was untrustworthy, she made preparations to ensure that she did not have to depend on him to go back and forth to work. Each morning, she would start her day early and catch the bus with her baby, dropping her at the daycare before her start time. The job proved to come easy, and she excelled at everything she did. The arguing between Adaoma and Marco continued, and her home life with him soon became as miserable as her childhood once was. She soon decided to save up her money to get an apartment of her own. Since Marco was quick to say he would kick her out, this would be the best solution to their problems.

When Adaoma told Marco that she would move out, he agreed it was a good idea. She had grown cold and would rarely let him touch her at this point in their relationship. She knew he was sleeping with other women but did not mind. Better them than her, she thought. Unfortunately, on some nights, he would still beg and plead to her for sex; on one of these occasions, he had an "oops." He had never made one mistake in the years she had been with him. When the first child was conceived, they had both agreed, so she knew this time was intentional. She would later learn that he had been tracking her cycle and knew exactly when she was ovulating. He knew her body better than she did.

At first, Adaoma was livid, but as the pregnancy progressed, she accepted the thought of the new baby and said that at least her two kids would have the same father. She knew how people talked about women with multiple baby daddies. Women were judged harshly, while the men were free to populate the earth and leave babies everywhere they went. This was the way it was.

During her pregnancy, she grew to despise Marco even more. He rarely picked her up from work on time, and she had to wait hours with their daughter for a ride home. Sometimes she would just ride the bus, but it was very hard with a stroller and being pregnant. One day, she saw a pregnant lady get on the bus with five kids. She saw her own life flash before her eyes and just how easy it was to get caught up. It had now been seven years since she moved in with

Marco, and the life they had was not what she wanted for herself. She began to develop her exit strategy.

The second baby arrived, and Adaoma moved when the new baby was just three months old. She found an apartment not far away from her job, which was perfect! Living on her own with two children was hard but manageable. She was finally at peace. Marco would come to see the kids often, and, at first, everything seemed cool. But then he changed. He soon realized that he did not like taking care of his oldest daughter by himself and that life was harder for him without her. He would try to guilt her by saying that Maria missed her and her sisters.

By now, Adaoma was an adult and would not fall for his manipulation. She would tell him that she refused to raise her children in a house of chaos and that they argued too much. Her children would never know what it was like to live with parents who always fought. When his trickery didn't work, he would cry and beg. At first, she thought he was joking because, in all the years, he never once even said that he loved her. He could not be serious, she thought. He then called her a heartless bitch for not giving in to his manipulation and began to stalk her. For months after her move, he would harass her and follow her. When he wasn't cursing her out and calling her sluts and whores, he was crying and begging her to come back. It became a routine that would be repeated time and time again.

With her newfound freedom and Marco's erratic behavior, she still managed to finally learn how to drive. She immediately bought herself a nice, new car and no longer had to catch the bus. She would have it for a month before Marco put sugar in the gas tank. She confronted him, and of course, he denied it. His next step would be calling her at her job and harassing her to the point where she was eventually fired. In his mind, she would have to come back now. Instead, she found another job, replaced her engine, and put a lock on her gas tank. She was determined.

Marco, at one time, had so much control over her life that he could not believe it was gone forever, and that was when he snapped. It was the weekend, and Marco was to pick up the kids, and again, he started with the begging, and again, she refused. He then pulled out a long knife and began chasing her down the street. Adaoma's heart beat fast as she ran for her life. In a flash, she remembered the story of how her own granddaddy had stabbed her grandmother in the head and cut her intestines out of her stomach. All while her mother was only an infant. Her grandmother lay in a pool of blood while their newborn baby cried on the bed next to her. It was because Grandma had refused to take him back after years of abuse. Her grandmother told her how she had begged for her life and that he had shown no mercy. Grandma was lucky to have survived.

At that moment, Adaoma stopped running and turned to face him. With every bit of courage in her tiny body, she looked him dead in the eyes and said, "I'd rather die than live the rest of my life in misery with you."

Marco lunged at her, but suddenly he changed his mind. Maybe he realized that he would spend most of his days in prison. Maybe he decided he did not want his children to grow up without a mother or father. Or maybe he had finally accepted that the control he once held over the young, naïve, barely 16-year-old girl was gone forever.

To this day, she still wonders what would have happened had she not stood up to this man who was three times her size and 11 years older than her. A man who should have looked at her like a child instead of as an opportunity. She wonders what life would be like for the two beautiful young women she raised by herself, who now have children and families of their own. To this day, she wonders what made Marco change his mind. Oh, how she still wonders.

Chapter 4

Choosing Your Partner

L et's go way back & revisit **Chapter 1** and your assignment to write down what you want in a mate. By now, you should have an "idea" of what you want at this stage in your life, so now it's time to prepare yourself to know how to recognize him when he arrives. Remember, we need to be extremely honest with ourselves in determining who would be a suitable mate for "us," and this takes experience and knowledge. My hope for you is that you have to kiss a minimal number of toads to get to your prince.

When getting to know someone, most women go into the situation with their guard up. They tend to arrive fully armored, and as time goes on, these layers are slowly peeled away. Men know this, which is why it takes a while for them to show you their authentic selves. As mentioned, come prepared to meet the representative and, if you like him, be open to meeting the real him when the time is right. Keep in mind, as a lady, you should always protect your heart, but at the same time, you do not want to be so guarded that you forget how to enjoy the thrill and pleasures that come with dating and meeting someone new and exciting.

Bear in mind that a wise woman always has a certain mystique about her, and men are attracted to the unknown. While learning your newfound interest, don't let him get you into a routine too soon and keep parts of your life a mystery to him. Don't answer every time he calls right away, or you will appear as if you will always be at his beck and call. Remember, in no form or fashion should you ever come off as completely naive. Also, know that some men will attempt to take advantage of the appearance of inexperience and to always stand by your own convictions while being open to being swayed in your beliefs only when new information is introduced and confirmed.

As we know these days, choosing a partner is no longer one size fits all type of deal. At one time, it was basically the following for African American women in the U.S.:

- Is he Black? ✓
- Does he have a job? ✓
- Is he likely to be a good provider? ✓
- Do my parents approve? ✓
- Do I like him enough to start a family with him? ✓

Hooray! If the man checked all the boxes above, you were most likely on your way to the altar. Most of our grandparents, and some of our parents, were just trying to get out of the house, and that was the only objective. Seriously, the goal at one time was to simply get married, buy a house and have a family! Can you believe that? Insert hysterical laugh here.

Nowadays, we are more inspired to look for someone to go on this life journey with. Some men want what can be paraphrased as a ride-or-die chick (depending on his interpretation of such, we don't do that anymore), and some women want a man that can lead and teach them without hindrance, damage, and control. Nowadays, looking for a mate to build with and start (or blend) a family looks more like this:

- Does he have good credit?
- Has he been to prison, and if so, how long?
- If he has been to prison, did he come out wiser or damaged?
- Is he employable?
- Does he have a job?
- Is he trying to at least get a job?
- How much money does he make?

- Is he self-employed?

- If self-employed, is it a real company that pays taxes, etc., or is his business just delusions of grandeur?

- Is he a natural-born male? If not, does he have the equipment I desire?

- Does he have children from a previous relationship?

- How many baby mommas does he have?

- How much child support is he paying out?

- Are the baby mommas gonna try and fight me?

- Is he gonna try and fight or, worse, kill me?

- Is he addicted to video games?

- Is he addicted to drugs?

- Is he addicted to anything?

- Is he secretly bi-sexual or gay?

- If bi-sexual, will he want me to participate?

- Is he monogamous?

- Is he polyamorous?

- Does his dick work?

- If his dick doesn't work, how about his tongue?

- Does he have an STI?

- If he has an STI, is it one I can live with?

- Is he a cheater?

- Is he Black?

- If not Black, is he slightly racist?

- If not slightly racist, is he racist?

And the list goes on and on. I say these things only to point out that modern life has increasingly become more complex, and as a result, we have become more aware and, dare I say, picky. Dating sites often give the illusion that we have an endless supply of men to choose from, but unfortunately, that is not the case. Most of the candidates on those sites have already kissed a number of toads themselves, and many of the men are scorned, immature, toxic, and have a list of other attributes you want to avoid.

In actuality, there will be a very small percentage of men that you will meet who are even close to meeting most of your desires. For this reason and others, you cannot afford to fumble or overlook him. Yes, we know the decision is not entirely up to you, but at the same time, you must always remember that you have the **POWER.** You control who comes into your life. You control who has access to you.

Likes vs. Dislikes or Biases?

For one to be able to choose, one must first understand their likes/dislikes and biases while also being confident in knowing what works for them. In my past, there were times when a good-intended friend suggested that I date someone I normally would not and probably was not even attracted to. These encounters never led to anything close to appealing or exciting, for that matter. Being attracted to someone physically and intellectually are two very important aspects of dating, even for women.

In a patriarchal society, we are often fed the notion that men only need money to get women, and women only need to be attractive. In the cases of men, that may still hold some truth for some, to an extent. After all, who wants to date someone who can only take them to the corner store? But because the "Modern Woman" more than likely works and has her own money, for us, the fellas have to come with much more than that.

Ladies like myself also desire a decent-looking package, and some men are not pleased. The way I see it is that if my man desires that I be shapely and fit, then why should I not want the same? I would love to be half of a "beautiful" couple, wouldn't you? Don't get me wrong, there are plenty of beauty and the beast type duos who are perfectly happy, but the point is to be true to thy self and understand your likes and dislikes while still assessing the entire man, and not just a part of him.

My suggestion is to really get to know and understand your preferences and desires. It is true that sometimes ya gotta try some things to be certain that you don't like them, but as you mature and evolve, you will become more confident in your own assertions. So, if you are certain you do not like men you think are ugly, don't date ugly men. If you don't care for smokers, don't date smokers. Not into kids, don't date men with kids. If heavy-set dudes repulse you, don't try to ride the tsunami. No interest in short dick men, simply don't date short dick men. Haha! Now I know you are probably wondering how you would know until after that first sexual encounter. You may not know-know, but we will review some tips later when we go over our **Sex Life Matters Chapter** that will help give you some idea of what you may be in for before the first encounter.

The point is to just know that being with someone you don't like or are attracted to is a disservice to you and that other person. Remember, one woman's trash is another woman's treasure, so be mindful and do not hold someone else's match hostage, and even more importantly, don't allow someone to hold you hostage from your future mate. If he ain't the one, he ain't the one.

Choosing Your Partner

Likes	Dislikes	Possible Biases

Pimpette Chronicles

Likes	Dislikes	Possible Biases

So, It Is. But Never Was.

Carla, 44, had been alone for some time when she met A.J., 50, on a dating site for singles who loved to camp. Carla was a modern go-getter who had no children (nor desire to have any), and A.J. was a single father of one adult daughter. When they began talking, it was not long before the two were head over heels in love. They lived more than 700 miles from each other, but that did not stop them from dreaming of one day having a future together.

During the time of their online courtship, COVID-19 was running rampant, so not being able to touch and kiss was not so much of a big deal to them both. They both had been pretty much isolated for about a year now. Many lonely nights consisted of honest conversations about their needs, including sexual ones. Carla had just left a loveless, sexless relationship, so she knew exactly what she wanted in a mate. Since intimacy was very important to Carla, A.J. sent her dick pics to assure her that he had adequate equipment and that everything was intact. She was pleasantly impressed.

Once the flying restrictions were lifted, the first thing that A.J. wanted was to meet her in person. Although Carla lived alone, she was comfortable with having A.J. visit her. She had relatives living in the same neighborhood, and she was a woman who could handle her own if things were ever rough. Being skilled in Kickboxing and Jiu Jitsu, Carla could take down even the mightiest of men.

Unfortunately, A.J. missed his flight on the day of the trip. He had arrived at the airport too late and blamed it on a friend who had promised to take him. Carla knew this was a red flag and showed that he had poor planning skills, if nothing else. She firmly believed in having plans A, B, and C. She became suspicious and had he not video-chatted her from the airport, she would not have believed him.

A.J. then tried to get a refund to reschedule but said the airport would not give him his money back. He told her that all of his funds were "tied up" (code words for broke) and that he could not afford to simply buy another ticket. Carla felt sorry for him (and horny for herself) and offered to come to him instead. She had not been on a flight in years and had family nearby, so she would not be completely vulnerable. A.J. was worth the risk, she thought.

When she arrived at the airport, A.J. was anxiously waiting. He began to approach her, and she realized he was much shorter and smaller than he had appeared on camera. He was childlike in size and could have very well been able to shop in the children's section at any clothing store. He beamed like an x-mas tree while she worked to hide her disappointment. As he gave her a huge hug, her nostrils filled with the slight stench of must. She brushed it off because it was a very hot day, and he had probably been waiting for her for a while. A.J. happily grabbed her luggage and began to carry it to his car.

After sweating and walking what seemed like two city blocks, they finally reached his vehicle. She was shocked to see he drove an

98

old beat-up pickup truck and not the sports car he had shown her pictures of. He said it was in the shop and apologized for having to pick her up in something so inadequate. Carla had been taught early on not to judge a man based on material things, but still, she was a little taken back and uncomfortable in the *Sanford and Son* type of ride.

As they began the trip to his house, he excitedly told her how happy he was to see her. At this point, she started to remember what made her like him most, and it was his sparkling green eyes and charming personality. She relaxed a little and said to herself, "Well, he isn't so bad."

She was intrigued by the perfectly trimmed landscaping that showcased a unique rainbow of flowers as they pulled up to his home. She found the neatly painted bungalow quite fitting for his sleek hippie style. On the inside, the walls were covered in carefully chosen African art, and his home smelled of incense and cannabis. Carla was not much into smoking, but she did not mind or judge those who did. After all, it is much harder to find someone who does not smoke these days than to find someone who does, she thought.

While the two of them were relaxing in his dimly lit living room, A.J. leaned in closely and kissed Carla. He slowly slipped his tongue into her mouth, and the foul taste of Black and Milds filled her taste buds. She recoiled in disgust, and he immediately noticed. He leaned back and asked her what was wrong, and she hastily, yet confidently, told him that she could taste the cigar on his tongue.

He immediately went to the bathroom, brushed his teeth and mouth, and returned. She thought it was the perfect way to handle such a human mistake and did not judge him for it. They both laughed and tried again. Success. They commenced to the shower and bedroom, where Carla soon learned that A.J. struggled with erectile dysfunction. He assured her that it didn't happen all the time and was probably because he was nervous. Luckily for Carla, his head game was superb.

The next morning, Carla and A.J. lay in bed and began to discuss the future, as they had so many times before. A.J. then mentioned how he had lived in roughly twenty different states and could pretty much make a home anywhere. Carla asked him how he could move so freely when he had a child in his hometown. He then disclosed that he had not seen his daughter in more than 16 years. This came as a shocker since he had spoken of his daughter as if he had helped raise her. Carla was learning that there was more to him than meets the eye.

As the week progressed, more bombshells would be dropped. The next mind-boggling info she learned was that A.J. had been homeless at one time, to the point of living in his car and sleeping on benches. He'd impregnated 14 women in his lifetime (that he knew of) and had been in love 20 times! After noticing the confused look on Carla's face, A.J. asked her how many times she had been in love. Her answer was simply 2 ½.

During this five-day visit, additional details of his character and life kept flowing. Not only did she learn that sex was going to always be a struggle for them (A.J. assured her that this inconvenience came as men got older and she would get used to it), but she was shocked to find out that he also needed to smoke a joint with his coffee every morning, had a habit of chain smoking cigars, and, although she couldn't be sure, she suspected the rubber pussy she stumbled across probably contributed to his erectile dysfunction. After all, a real vagina definitely could not compete with a vibrating one.

Carla also found it to be quite "suspect" that everywhere they went, A.J. would point out the men who he said were "gay." She found this particularly peculiar since they had never discussed the LGBTQ+ community, and she had no idea why he thought she needed to know this information. Carla had learned more about him during this visit than she had learned in all the months they spent communicating virtually. By the end of the trip, she was unsure whether or not she wanted to continue the relationship and wondered if she was being "picky." She had been accused of this many times before.

The vacation away from home was pleasant enough as they enjoyed great outings that consisted of trips to the museum, national parks, trendy restaurants, and many other moderately inexpensive dates. On the last day with A.J., she took a good hard look at him and noticed the lines of age on his face, the despair in his eyes, and the advancing stages of tooth decay. Being a dental hygienist, Carla asked him when was the last time he had been to a dentist. He said it had been years.

For Carla, this knowledge gave insight into just how tough life had been for A.J. Most people know that when times are rough, the last thing you worry about is your teeth. Carla, since childhood, had always been extra careful with her own smile, and a man having a healthy smile was one of the things she absolutely required in a mate. From the looks of A.J.'s receding gums, she guessed his teeth had at most three years before they would start to exit stage left.

At that point, she knew that she and A.J. could never be. She severely disliked too many things about him, and the potential tooth loss was the icing on the cake. She had also realized that A.J. was a wanderer and was most likely looking for the next place to lay his head. Another major thing that concerned her was the number of times the condom would miraculously come off. She found herself thinking, "Is he trying to knock me up, too?" At a minimum, she felt if a man his age had not mastered a simple skill such as keeping a condom in place and had impregnated 14 women, he was a liability. She politely broke it off once she was in the safety of her own home.

About a year passed, and Carla decided to stalk A.J. via social media to see what he was up to. Remembering that she was infatuated with him for months during the pandemic, the reality was that he was special until he wasn't. She wasn't surprised to find that he had impregnated and moved in with a woman much younger than him who already had five other children, just a few months after he and Carla broke up.

The woman, she learned, had been divorced twice and could be considered lucky to find a man like A.J., who is unlikely to pursue future mates and would be happy to help raise her growing family. As with most men, A.J. certainly had "some" good qualities about him. But they were not the qualities that Carla needed or wanted in her life.

In the end, A.J. had succeeded in securing the roof over his head, and Carla was happy to have dodged that bullet. It was truly a win-win situation for them both. In all her emotional maturity, Carla had followed the cardinal rule of not holding someone else's match hostage, following her instincts, and not settling for less than what she truly wanted. Had she not decided to toss that fish back in the pond, she would not have been able to catch a bigger, more virile one.

The lesson from Carla's story is just how important it is that we choose wisely and do what is best for us and our future. Early in life, we all develop these things that we like and dislike, although some may change as we mature.

For example, let's say you grew up in a community where you witnessed people who drank alcohol, got drunk, cursed, and acted a fool. You would suspect that everyone who indulged would eventually exhibit these behaviors, and you would not like people who drank alcohol. Or if you were told that if you cursed, people would think you were unintelligent, you would not want to be around people who cursed, and you'd probably develop a bias against those who do. *Actually, scientific studies prove the complete opposite of those who like to slang an occasional F-bomb here and there, but if you grew up and was taught that, then not even science would likely change your mind.*

When seeking compatibility, these likes/dislikes, or in the last example, biases, can make or break the relationship. Work toward determining whether or not your preference is legit or if it is just a bias that was ingrained in you. Let's say you do not want to date men who drink alcohol because the smell and taste make you ill, and you hate to kiss a man with liquor on his breath. That would definitely be a legitimate enough reason to know that you do not like men who drink because this outcome will directly affect your intimate relationship with him. The point is to be confident in who you choose to spend your time with and understand your likes, dislikes, and biases.

Be sure to always create an expiration date on how much time you plan on investing in a situationship before you would need to move on if it is not progressing the way you believe it should, and there are things about the person that you do not like. Be honest and meticulous with how you move, and don't go in with the knowledge that you would never want to commit to that type of person, yet have them think there is a chance or, even worse, waste time trying to convince yourself. Don't misuse the "nice" guy who will do anything for you while you wait for a more compatible mate to come along. Be honorable and respectful in everything you do, and you won't have to worry about that bitch named Karma.

The Three Stages of Dating

As mentioned before, **dateable** simply means attractive in a romantic way; available for a date. To *"date"* is simply to arrange a social or romantic appointment. In the past, people dated to get to know someone to move closer to courtship and hopefully a relationship. Nowadays, the goals or agendas are as diverse as the people on this planet. If you ask someone what a date is, you will rarely find people who are in agreement. Some people think going over to someone's house to watch movies and chill is a date; others feel that meeting in public is a date, while many don't feel they have reached a date until they have shared an evening, which includes a meal.

Regardless of what you or I think a date is, the ultimate goal is usually the same for men and women. Both parties are looking for someone they can eventually have **SEX** with. The end. I know I just ruined the romantic part of it all, the excitement of meeting someone for the first time, the thrill of the first kiss, the romance in that first dance, blah blah blah…. But the fact remains that the other party wants to see you naked! Yes, men and women desire sex! Who knew? We knew…. That ain't a bad thing, is it? After all, "Sex is natural, sex is fun, not everybody does it, but everybody should," *George Michael, circa 1987.*

Some people are looking to have sex upon the first date, while others are looking for sex after some sort of dating process, whether it be the old-fashioned 90-day rule (which is a waste of time because everyone knows the rule) or after some other duration we have set up in our own mind. Needless to say, we all want it. When a woman agrees to go out with a man, it is usually because there is a chance that she "may" want to have sex with him. Now, once he gets to that first date, the rest is usually up to him. Even some of the most unattractive, unappealing men can find themselves between the thighs of a woman they probably have no right being in between. Timing is everything, and once those stars align, ain't nothing you can do about it.

Now, before you ladies go and give up some of your **POWER**, 'cause yes, Pussy is **POWER,** let's think about who you are giving it to. Since you have already read our ***Beware of the Bitter Man Section,*** you have an idea of just some of the types of men rampant in our community and also exactly where you may need to place them, if at all, in your life. The fact is that many men may not be "Good Men," but nonetheless, they are all usually good for something. Some of the fellas you may find yourself on a date with, you may simply just want to share one intimate night, and there is nothing wrong with that as long as everything is done honestly and safely. I mean, if he is dumb as a rock but has the body of a stallion, why not go for a ride?

For the others you may see potential in the long term, you never handle the same as the "stallions" for numerous reasons. This is not to say that you cannot get to know him and maybe even have sex on the first in-person date without it growing into something more than a one-night stand. That has happened to many people I have talked to on more than one occasion. Hell, my longest-running one-nighter lasted two years. The point is, when you feel the time is right, the time is right, but proceed with caution. Once you can no longer negotiate the value of your vagina, it's hard to make that sell.

It has been my opinion, and that of most men that I have talked to, that regardless of when a woman decides to share her body with them, most men value what they have to work for the most. I know, this sounds like a game, and you just want to be honest and not play any games and all that jazz, so I am sorry to be the one to tell you: life is a game in all aspects of the definition, which by the way is "**a form of play or sport, especially a competitive one played according to**

rules and decided by skill, strength, or luck." If you are still one of those folks wandering through life, not recognizing that this is just a game, more power to you. I will be sure to write a subsequent book breaking that down in the future, but until then, just take my word for it.

Once you get past the dating process (if that is your goal), the next step is naturally courting. Traditionally courting meant dating someone with the intent of marrying. Now, if you look up the word, you will see various definitions of what it means. Some include marriage, while others do not. Since more and more people are choosing not to marry, I believe that the more appropriate and modern definition would be along the lines of "when a couple is getting to know each other to see if they are a fit." Courting is about developing a bond to see if this is your partner for however long you two decide to be together.

In the past, men who were interested in a lady did certain things to show their level of interest and the seriousness of the pursuit. Currently, we live in a dating climate where some women feel that they must also court the man. How many times have you heard a woman bragging and telling other women that the car he drives, she bought for him, or that the clothes he wears she provided? Ladies these days will happily pay for haircuts, gym shoes, etc., for a dude they know is sleeping with other women. #Goofy.

As for me and my Pimpettes, we are not about that life. But that ain't my business. Honestly, I cannot begin to understand how a woman can expect a man to "lead" and be the head of the household, all while she is making him feel like a lady and taking care of him.

Truthfully, many men have always been nothing more than pure figureheads in the household, but for our purposes, those are not the types of men we want to attract, nor the types of relationships we want to curate. With this basic knowledge in place, I will advise against courting the man. It simply sends out the message that he is the prize and you are pursuing him. With the numbers already stacked against us as Black women seeking Black men, this usually leads to our men getting courted by many women, which could leave you out in the cold with a bitter heart and a wet ass.

The relationships previously mentioned are not goals in any sense of the word, so if he is unsure about you, let her have him. Save yourself the pain of a lover who will likely spend years between you and the other women on his roster. Those men rarely, if ever, completely stop messing with other women. They are accustomed to having too many options, so you being the chosen one who is married to one of them, will be no walk in the park. Men who have been coddled and overly fed by women in their lifetime usually only stop messing around with other chicks when they are old, and their dicks barely work.

So, ask yourself, are you really missing out if the best you can snag is a dude who is not head over heels in love with you and treats you like you are an asset in his life? Trust and believe that a man who cares for you will likely do anything to keep you, and he will not pit you against other women because he would not want to hurt you. Anyone who makes you feel that you have to compete to gain his affection, love, and trust is undoubtedly not worth the sorrow.

To double back, understand that I am not saying showing interest should not be reciprocal because it definitely should be. Reciprocation can be little acts of kindness and being available to spend time with him, following up with him, asking him how he is doing, being supportive, and very "small" tokens of affection, etc. For example, surprise him with his favorite brownie from the bakery or buy him a set of glasses for his kitchen if you notice he does not have any. Pay attention to the things he enjoys and some of the needs in his life that he may have neglected. Here you may have spent about $20 when a date can easily cost anywhere from $130 on up for two people (assuming you ain't paying for these dates). You're not, right, sis?

Anyway, multiply that by the number of continuous dates in comparison to those little tokens to show you care, and that my darling is an inexpensive investment. The point is, it is his job to court and win you over, not the other way around. As I've heard before, some women say the competition is fierce and that women are doing anything to get a man. I've met (and sent on their way) some of these men, and honey, they usually ain't nothing that you should want to call your own. Once a good man wins you over, and you are **his woman,** then what you choose to do for him is **unlimited.**

In addition, if the fella has not made it clear that he wants to be with you and that his goal is to make you his woman, then keep dating until you meet one who does. When I say "clear," that means not only verbally but also in action. For example, spending quality time with you outside the bedroom, taking you out, spending money on you, asking about you and your life, etc. A man who wants you will do everything within his power to please and keep you, so recognize the ones who do from the ones who do not.

OK, now the next stage after courting is the relationship. At this point, you are both "all in," and you begin planning your future together. This may include legal marriage or a non-traditional route, such as cohabiting or simply being in a partnership. Be aware that people will always put pressure on folks to get married, but marriage is not for all, nor does it guarantee that a relationship will stay in place.

Statistically, it's more likely to fail than succeed, but that does not mean you shouldn't try at least once, in my opinion, "if" that is your desire. Marriage, when done right, can be one of the most glorious partnerships on the planet. Although the jury is out on whether or not I personally want to marry again, I still envy some of the seasoned couples who appear to have a great marriage. I know that many of these folks have been through many trials and tribulations, but nonetheless, they are admirable.

My view on legal marriage is that it should be more about protecting assets than love. When people are invested in the union emotionally and financially, they are not so quick to call it quits. Nowadays, people get married, and sometimes those partners become more of a hindrance and liability than an asset. If you are not planning on building wealth, protecting assets, or gaining some sort of security—whether it is to just ensure that you can get the other person's retirement, insurance money, pension, 401K, or whatever assets they leave behind in the event of death—then you do not have to be married to have a full, complete, beautiful relationship. It is your choice, so do what is best for your life!

Marrying someone when there is not necessarily an issue of protecting assets or the home you two may have built together and then having that relationship go bad can become an unnecessary nightmare. It's much harder to sever that contract for so many reasons. The divorce process can be expensive and tedious. There are often feelings of time lost, failure, and inadequacies because, in effect, it can be viewed as a failed business venture. There is the cost of starting over and the inconvenience of moving out of a place you call home, and let's not forget that awkward time of simply getting back into the dating scene.

This transitionary period can become expensive and complicated for both parties involved as they struggle to find balance in life and separate assets. Some decide to just stay in the marriage because the divorce process can become so complex. So again, marriage is not always the cherry on top. I would rather be in a committed relationship, where both parties are there because they want to be and not because they have to be.

What Exactly Is a Good Man?

Many things we experience and are told truly shape how we choose our mates. Depending on the age and mindset of a person, reshaping perspectives can be a daunting task. Considering who may have shaped their perception—their momma, daddy, or mentor—that person may be held in such a regard that they cannot fathom the possibility that the information received is null and void.

Women usually tend to be much more open to new information, which is part of the reason we crave men who can teach us something. Unfortunately, we are too easily influenced by the men in our lives, which is also why we often find it hard to maintain our own autonomy once in partnership. When choosing a mate, it is best to share your life with someone you can learn from without him crushing or inhibiting who you are.

We must always be on the lookout for men who try to make us feel like we have to be something other than who we are, to fit into their idea of a perfect match. In partnership, people need to understand that no one will ever be 100 hundred percent of what you think a mate should be, but they should come so close that the rest seems unimportant. In the end, the person you choose should make you feel like a queen inside and out.

The King and Queen - Trigger Warning - Abuse

I once knew a woman who had been abused by most men around her since childhood. When she grew up and started dating, she thought that any man who did not do the things her abusers did was a "good man." Her past experiences of sexual trauma, helplessness, and pain gave her an indication of how she did not want to feel, but not necessarily a good healthy foundation for how she should feel while being safe and loved. As she grew older, she met a suave man who began to pursue her. He showered her with compliments, gifts, and small tokens of gratitude while praising her publicly in front of friends and family. She, in return, would learn to do the same, and together they called themselves King and Queen.

In the beginning, everything was wonderful. She became comfortable enough to share the details of her horrid past, a past that her family members had taught her to keep secret, and he pumped her full of new knowledge and information. He also encouraged her to speak up about her pains while offering the support and reassurance she had failed to find elsewhere. He would tell her that she was a strong, powerful Black woman and more brilliant than anyone he had ever met. She would get high off of his praise and would soon learn that speaking about her trauma gave her a sense of empowerment, and he became a huge part of her growth.

The positive feelings that she would feel around him were so strong that her entire self-esteem was wrapped around what he thought of her. It was not long before she became a mirror image of his likeness and spoke of him as if he was a god. Even when he was not around, her sentences would often start with what he told her, what he thought and felt she should do. He was her protector, the one she'd never had as a child.

Together they built a family and spoke earnestly of Black Power and liberation. She supported all of his failed business endeavors while working two jobs to support their family, which consisted of numerous children from his previous relationships. He, in turn, pursued his aspirations of being a great speaker, leader, and pillar of the community. He spoke in the streets of male leadership while she paid all of the bills at home, and he lived practically free in the house she had bought before meeting him. Eventually, she became pregnant and bore him healthy twin boys.

Once the children were born, this King's true nature began to rear its ugly head. He no longer would listen to her horror stories of abuse and even told her she must have enjoyed being raped since she spoke of it so often. The compliments began to lessen and were replaced with criticisms. When the King spoke of his dissatisfaction with her, she would work twice as hard to regain his approval. If his business ventures fell apart, he would blame her for his inadequacies. If sex was unsatisfactory, he would tell her the cheating was her fault.

The relationship soon became a series of extreme highs and lows, where one moment he publicly praised her and the next he privately belittled her. As time dragged on, he one day announced that it was time to expand his tribe. Although they had discussed from the beginning that she only wanted two boys, and he had agreed, he now felt it was his duty and obligation as a Black man to further populate the earth. His now eight children were simply not enough. It was time for her to give him another offspring, he demanded while saying that he would be strengthening the Black nation by spreading his seed. When she resisted his desire to impregnate her, he would grow angry, yell and tell her that she was not about building and uplifting the community like he thought she was. Her King had become her nightmare.

After time passed and she refused to get pregnant, he announced that he would move his faithful concubine into the home that they shared, and she would be the one to bear him another child. They would become sister wives, and this would make their home run smoother. The King told his queen that this was a compromise and solution to their dilemma.

The Queen then told him that she was no longer happy in the relationship and that it would be better if he just moved out. Shocked that she was standing her ground, he refused and told her he was never leaving, and the only way to get rid of him was through death.

At this point, she began to take a good hard look at this man and her life. Her credit was shot from supporting his business ventures. She was always sad and crying. He often stayed out all night, so she was lonely. She was always worried about him getting angry, and to top it all off, she had become the primary parent for all of his children, including the ones that were not hers. She realized that these feelings of pain and inadequacy were not new to her. She then began to see that she now felt as helpless and trapped as she did as a child. Is this truly what having a good man feels like, she asked herself?

Since she had no real role model to show and teach her how a good man treats his woman, her vision was warped. It could be said that her perspective of men had been tainted at a young age, so this made her a target for this manipulator. All the "King" had to do was give her a false sense of power; he knew she would blindly follow him.

Recognizing that her sense of self-worth had been stripped as a child, he preyed on controlling her while appearing to want to empower her. Ultimately, the only person he wanted to empower was himself. This is yet another example of why inner-work is so important. By dealing with past traumas and knowing yourself, no one will be able to come into your life and manipulate your self-worth. Had this woman conquered her past pains, she would not have tried so hard to win and keep his approval.

At this point, I want you to define the qualities that you consider would make a good man and, even more importantly, think about how you believe a good man will make you feel. Here are some of the qualities that I look for in a potential mate and those that I look to avoid. Remember, your list should consist of the things that are important to YOU!

Good Qualities	Not So Good
Thoughtful, Honest	Inconsiderate, Sneaky, Dishonest
Generous, Caring, Giving	Selfish, Cheap, Petty
Loyal	False Hearted, Unfaithful, Cheater, Whorish
Helpful, Asset	Useless, Dead Weight, Hindrance, Liability
Sincere	Overly Apologetic, Manipulative
Peaceful	Chaotic, Temperamental, Angry, Anxious
Clean & Neat	Nasty, Junky, Disorganized
Logical	Unable to Critically Think, Close-minded
Attentive	Self-absorbed

Choosing Your Partner

Mature & Classy	Old, Egotistical, Boorish
Balanced	Sporadic
Exciting	Boring
Patient	Inpatient, Condescending
Intelligent, Wise	Unknowledgeable, Naive

Good Qualities	Not So Good

In addition, let's explore some things that do not automatically make a man a good match. When men use these as selling points, you really need to ask yourself the whys. Don't immediately assume the examples below make him a catch! Some will try to convince you they do because they have very little to offer, and they feel since there isn't much competition, you should not aim high. Remember, the only way to raise the bar is by demanding more.

When he tells you this	This could be why…
He brags about being monogamous and thinks this alone makes him a catch.	He could just desire one woman at a time or: He is a lousy or lazy lover. Struggling with erectile dysfunction etc Women seldom go back for seconds or stick around long. He has a micro penis.
He does not have kids, and he is over 35.	He is honestly just waiting for the right woman, or: Very picky/too picky Has already impregnated numerous women, and once they got to know him better, they did not want to be tied to him indefinitely and aborted the pregnancies.

	He can be sterile. Don't automatically assume it's by his choice.
He calls every day, all day.	He is very into you, or: Unemployed, has no life and will want it to be just you and him all of the time. He is clingy.
Been at the same job for 20+ years.	Loves stability and has grown in his position or: He has no ambition, is lazy, or has no other skill set.
He brags about being a heterosexual Black man.	Too ignorant to know that's nothing to brag about, or: He's bi, gay, or worried he is not heterosexual, which is why he keeps telling you that he is He wants to ensure you cannot tell he's attracted to men, too.

What is a Successful Relationship?

In the past, people viewed a successful relationship as one where both parties stayed together through good times and bad. Generations ago, women were taught that love endures, which meant that they would go through a series of trials and pains that were often laid out by the person who was supposed to love them. They were taught that most men could not control their urges and that it was natural for them to sow their oats. Even in current times, it is not uncommon for men to intentionally put women through a sequence of tests (which sometimes involve other women), with marriage to them being the reward.

Some of these women knowingly accept the bad behavior for years, hoping he would pick her in the end. The men often chose the one who proved that she would be there through thick and thin, even when infidelity and disrespect were a part of the package. I even knew a man who had behaved this way, married the woman who accepted the bad behavior, and then could not understand why she completely changed once she had a ring on her finger. This is what we call "the set up."

There is a special type of woman who is willing to sit on the pot for years and never take a shit just to get the man she wants. She knows that the other women will eventually lose interest or grow tired of the back and forth. Because so many men harbor what some may consider abandonment issues, from either an unresolved trauma in their family life or their first heartbreak, he may not recognize that this is why the "pick me" chick is so appealing.

Men who suffer from this type of damage look for women who are willing to do anything to prove to them that they will stay. They look for this safety, and when the relationship goes sour, which they usually do, they don't understand why she is tripping since she won the prize. For one thing, sir, she probably has an array of pent-up anger for all those times you made her cry, embarrassed, or disrespected her. In the end, no amount of stating "that's my wife" will ever make up for the things he may have done to her over the years.

Make no mistake, most women can become vengeful, resentful creatures to the core. Even those who seem timid and meek will wait patiently to get their revenge on one who has continuously crossed her. Where she once sat quietly at the family functions while his sister's friend, whom he was fucking, was just inches away, she is now cursing out the sister's friend, the sister, the cat, the dog, and everybody who has been talking shit about her for years. Remember, some forgive, but not everyone forgets.

Now, this husband has to support all of her shenanigans because it is long overdue, and he knows it. He is just happy when her wrath is focused on others instead of him. He may even join in on the drama because he knows this will win her approval and in no way does he want her to leave. Believe me when I say men desire stability and familiarity above all things, even more so than love. Men are typically lazy when it comes to finding a mate, and they are most likely to try to look for a way to make a relationship work with the woman they have and know.

This is also why so many men nowadays have side chicks. The wives often won't, or rarely, sleep with their husbands because, after all of the disappointments over the years, it becomes hard for her to even be attracted to him. Have you ever become so disappointed in a lover that you could no longer look them in the eyes? It's like you are only able to see past them and no longer see them. It is often said that you cannot expect the same love after you have continuously broken a heart. Personally, if you know you have done some major damage,

I think it is better if you just start anew with another person. Take those lessons and run.

The reality is that most men will not leave their wives, even when they are miserable. Some will spend the rest of their days trying to undo the past in hopes that, somehow, he will make her happy and she will forget. Yes, everyone is aware of the bull granddad put granny through and all those outside babies in the streets. This is also why we see those types of older men constantly praising their wives. They know their dicks no longer work, and it is next to impossible to get a new woman on board a sinking ship.

Many of our ancestors stayed in miserable or unfulfilling relationships for various reasons, including familiarity, fear of the unknown, finances, health issues, familial ties, children, or simply because they had no desire to start over. So, the question is, is it better to be with the devil you know than the devil you do not? I guess it depends on the type of life you want and whether or not happiness and peace are important.

Another problem with the woman who will accept anything in the relationship to get the man is that those women are generally not the type that will also encourage him to meet his greatest potential. The pick-me types are well suited for men with no real ambition, drive, or plans for the future. These men know that she will never demand much from him, so there is little chance that he will disappoint her. Talk about low expectations.

We often hear that a man's success is determined by the type of woman he marries, which is true. But oh, if it only worked both ways. It has been my experience that most men (not all) hinder a woman's growth. Our success has very little to do with whether or not he is there cheering us on. Black women, in particular, have been taught from childhood to be independent and work hard. Many of us did not grow up where we saw the man making it easier for the mothers; instead, we were likely exposed to the opposite.

Everyone goes into a relationship hoping they are successful together, but who determines what success looks like? I was once married to a decent man, and I remember how folks responded upon finding out that we had divorced. Some even told me how sorry they were. It always confused me because our divorce was a mutual decision that did not require a lawyer's involvement, and I was happy it was over. I was once even told that he and I were the only two people who had parted ways maturely, without bashing each other, that my relatives had ever witnessed.

I'm not saying that we didn't have our fair share of arguments, but at that stage in life, I had already mastered the skill of developing an **exit strategy.** Even when we argued, I maintained a certain level of respect and distance, making it nearly impossible for him to have anything negative to say or do to me. I waited until we were completely separated before I started dating and never once cheated while in the relationship.

The deterioration of our relationship had more to do with our inability to discuss problems maturely and come to a solution as a team. We'd spent many great years together, and when our relationship was no longer beneficial to us both, we ended it. To me, that was a successful relationship. There was no anger; there was no "he did this to me" or "she did that to me." We had simply come to the end of the road for many reasons, which both of us, at the time, did not feel were worth working to remediate. He did not leave me with scars or bruises, neither internal nor external, and I walked away wiser and more confident in my ability to survive and assert my needs in the next relationship.

Somewhere in time, people started feeling like they had to make the other person out to be a villain in order to exit a relationship. Some think that a breakup gives them the right to become an assassin of the other person's character. We often get caught up in trying to make ourselves look innocent while attempting to make the other person look bad.

Honestly, many of us worry entirely too much about what people outside of the relationship think about our lives and partners. It takes two people to make or break a relationship, and there really is cause and effect for everything we do. Break-ups do not have to be dramatic endings every time you sever a relationship. Sometimes, you can dip out when you know in your heart it is simply time to go. A successful relationship, in the end, can include the following and more:

- You two are dedicated to maintaining and meeting each other's needs.

- Whether emotional or sexual, you are dedicated to being together to the end or until you are both unable to meet each other's needs.

- You have developed a goal together, and you are both dedicated to seeing it achieved.

- You two have evolved in different ways, and now, at this stage in your lives, you feel it would be best to separate. Your decision most likely has nothing to do with an outside force or person, but if it does, you are honest and respectful with your partner and will not do anything to destroy their trust.

- You did not cause harm to the other person's reputation, and vice versa, upon the exit.

- You two have children together, and the main objective is to ensure that all of their needs are met, whether you are in a partnership or not. The objective never changes, even if the relationship does.

- You two have raised a healthy individual even though you are no longer together, and you can come together during graduations, weddings, etc., with mutual respect.

All of the above should be considered a successful relationship. A successful relationship, again, does not include a lifetime of pain, misery, or disappointment. Relationships should bring you joy, happiness, and pleasure. Of course, there will be rainy days, but how you handle and deal with them will ultimately break or make the relationship.

Chapter 5

Dating in the New Millennium

Never Give Up All of Your POWER!

Before I got back into these mean dating streets, I was in a committed relationship that lasted over six years. Comfortable in my security, I gained over 30 pounds and was borderline of having high cholesterol. Years of sitting down at a desk at work, toppled by a lack of regular aerobic activities (including sex), had begun to take their toll. My fiancé and I had simply allowed the familiarity of everyday life and pressures at the job to break our intimate bond while destroying our bodies. We had both been in pretty good shape when we met, but now we were both thick as hell.

Growing up, cooking was always one of my passions and a part of my personality. I loved preparing meals for my family and friends and enjoyed seeing the joy a home-cooked meal brought to their faces. In this relationship, my partner did not understand how important it was for me to sit down and share a meal with him.

Oftentimes, he would come home to dinner and tell me he would eat later, leaving me to dine alone. When our kids were at home, I spent weekends baking and preparing meals they would share with me, but those days had come and gone. It was now just the two of us, and things had drastically changed.

After the first two years of being an empty nester, my primary motherly role had mostly disappeared, and it was time for some adaptations. Eventually, I left my office job and returned to film production and gig work. The work was stressful but fun, and I enjoyed the freedom of meeting exciting people. Meanwhile, at home, I began to accept that the relationship was over and it was time to move on.

Unfortunately, the gig work was not consistent, and I was not earning the amount of money required to move out on my own. My then fiancé said he did not care what I did outside of the home, giving me the OK to seek affection elsewhere. My character would not allow me to be the type of woman who could feel comfortable going out, seeing someone else, and then returning to sleep in "our" home. I was saddened that he expected this of me, and he had grown content with our current state of being. We had truly hit rock bottom.

For months, the lonely nights continued that featured me eating alone and him becoming engulfed in his virtual video games. Sometimes, he would go days without speaking to me when he was angry. Other times, he would nitpick everything I did, and it seemed nothing was ever perfect enough in the home. If I vacuumed, he would come behind me and vacuum again. If I washed dishes, he would reorganize them. This drove me crazy, and I felt like a trapped animal, which looking back, seems quite suitable since, at that stage in my life, my partner had begun to treat and look at me as if I were some sort of pet.

To be clear, all of my basic needs were met, but I was not looked at as a woman, lover, or asset to his life. Though no physical abuse, the mental abuse began to weigh heavy on my soul. When I would complain about the things lacking in our relationship, he would simply say most women would be happy to be where I was. After all, I was a kept woman, so that was all that mattered, right?

With all of my skills, knowledge, and quite frankly, good pussy, I had been reduced to something pretty he could come home to after a grueling day at work, and I'd be there to ignore or for him to direct his frustrations upon. I soon found myself wondering if there was something wrong with me since he no longer seemed to find me attractive. This was a very lonely stage in my life, but many of my friends kept telling me I might as well stay where I was because there were simply few viable men out there, and he was a great catch!

One thing's for sure, my Grandma Lucinda had taught me early in life that a man was like a bus, and if you miss one, another would be along soon after. I refused to believe the "ain't no good men out here" theory. Honestly, in all my years of "dating," I truly have never missed a beat, so grannie's advice has always reigned true.

The final straw, and what ultimately forced me to move my feet, was when my ex and I were having a conversation, and the topic was, what would happen if he were to die suddenly? Where would I live if he were to pass since the house that we lived in was in his name only? Now, mind you, I had put my blood, sweat, and tears into making it our home, too, which included picking it out and handling all of the business aspects involved with the purchase.

I had coordinated and initiated all of the remodeling and upkeep, inside and out, and there was not an inch within this 2,000-square-foot bungalow, where I had not helped scrape walls, paint, or lay the vinyl flooring. In the beginning, our teamwork worked well; he would pay for almost anything I wanted to make our home beautiful, and I had the freedom to decorate and change things as I saw fit. It was not uncommon for him to come home and find that I had painted an entire room in a day. But since we were never married, his assets and this home were simply not mine.

Although I paid a small portion of our bills, he was the primary breadwinner and head of the household. When he would answer the question of what would happen if he passed, he simply said that if he died, the house would go to his adult daughter, who no longer lived with us and had a house of her own, and I would have to work something out with her to stay in the place I called home. This was the answer to a question that told me everything I needed to know about the relationship.

I imagined myself growing older, in a sexless, joyless relationship, only to be tossed out on the streets in my older years. I am not sure how he thought this would be OK with me, but since we were not married, this was totally within his rights. Please know that no matter how much we want to romanticize it, marriage is simply a business contract designed to protect assets.

Since I had decided that the benefits of marriage would not outweigh the risks in this relationship, I had long since abandoned the idea of signing a contract. Apparently, he did not care or understand that a man who truly loves his woman would want her to be able to survive without begging in the event of his demise. Since he had no intention of ensuring I was protected, it was my responsibility to protect myself. It was time to move on.

Looking back, I do not regret my time in that relationship because it served my children and me well. Most of the years were happy, and he and I managed to remain friends. When we met, we needed each other to grow as people.

Although I was in a less-than-ideal situation, in the end, one thing I had learned early on in life that prepared me for that moment was to never give up all of my **POWER**. As fate would have it, my tenants would soon inform me that they were moving out of my rental home, which enabled me to prepare to move in. The ability to be able to pick up my bag and say "deuces" is inevitably what saved me from not missing a beat.

Social Media and Dating

As we know, social media has given us access to people we normally would never have the chance to meet in real life. Through dating apps, we can simply swipe left or right when a person grabs our attention in hopes that the feeling is mutual. We have no problem putting on a smiley face while proclaiming that we deserve to be the object of his or her affection. Well, at least for the time being.

Historically, in the U.S. and many other countries, men have always enjoyed the pleasure of being able to pursue multiple women at one time. It has only been most recently that women can now also indulge in such activities. Nowadays, many men and women are deciding to remain single because the risks often do not outweigh the benefits.

Due to the endless amount of seeming options, people these days are quick to bail out when things are not going the way they feel they should. When asked, here is a list of some of the challenges that people encounter while dating that make it hard for them to stay in the game:

Dating in the New Millennium

1. Dating too much. Some men and women will date people they know they are not compatible with or have no interest in, just to be on a date. For example, dating out of boredom, loneliness, or hunger. **Please stop doing that shit!**

2. Dating apps are not selective enough. Profiles do not do a thorough job of screening potential suitors for the individual.

3. Dating apps are being used like a menu. For example, this weekend, I would like to meet a muscular city boy with locks. Next week, I'll have a clean-shaven country dude. This excess access is becoming problematic, and the behavior is leading to quick emotional and sexual fixes.

4. The woman creating a profile immediately puts herself in a position where she is an option and not a priority. Please note that we all have options, but should you really be made to feel like one?

5. Pre-date conversations with men you meet on dating apps are often a waste of time. That first screening call could last over an hour, and then you may have just wasted time on someone you may never even meet.

6. A lot of people on dating sites are purely looking for someone to talk to with little to no interest in ever meeting the person. **Beware, a lot of these men are lonely as fuck nowadays!**

7. Men have become passive in pursuing women. They sit back and wait for you to do the courting but then "ask" you to let them lead. P.S., if he has to ask, he probably isn't capable. **#Weak.**

8. Men complain women are too aggressive but then sit back and complain if the woman does not pursue them. Huh?

9. Lack of sexual alignment. For example, he can't perform for physical reasons, simply lacks the equipment needed, or he is into some kinky shit you aren't into.

10. They lie about height, weight, marital status, income, everything.

11. Burnt out on dating, and now looking at everyone like they are the same. Self-sabotage.

With all these challenges and more, it's a miracle that two people ever come together long enough to develop a relationship, get married, and stay married. The convenience of finding someone in your community who is looking for a romantic partner without having all of the guesswork that used to take place when people met in person has, as mentioned previously, commodified our relationships. The problem has arisen so swiftly that getting people back on track will take some serious damage control. The first step is to get out of the fast-food dating scene and develop your own list of detailed standards and requirements.

Raising the Bar!

It is no secret that there is a gender imbalance amongst African Americans in terms of finding a suitable mate. Black men nowadays will outright tell you they are a catch simply because they are heterosexual Black male who has not been in prison. Hell, even the ones who have been in the slammer for a spell will try and convince you that they are the prize. I am not saying that prison automatically eliminates someone from being a man of quality. I know some very honorable Black men who any woman would be lucky to call their own, who have been incarcerated, but do the aforementioned qualities automatically make a man a great catch? I think not! In this day and age, we definitely need to aim much higher than that.

Living in the H.P.

Andrea lived in a small town in Metro Detroit called H.P., which is about a three-mile radius. She'd been born and raised in the H.P. At 50 years old, she never even dated a man outside her community. She had settled into a life of long-term on-and-off-again relationships with men she had grown up with. Any man who was not similar to the guys Andrea knew from her hood simply did not appeal to her, yet she wondered why she could never develop a healthy, monogamous relationship with these dudes.

Most women in her hood were pretty similar to Andrea, and the neighborhood fellas just rotated them throughout the decades. The ladies were usually somewhat educated, held good jobs, and had some sort of security. On the other hand, the men who never left the community rarely kept a steady job, were in and out of prison and had multiple children with different women. In comparison, the women usually only had a few children by the same man, and it was rare to see multiple baby daddies in these familial units. So, in actuality, the men were causing the broken homes, broken hearts syndrome, and simply planting their seeds wherever they could lay their heads, usually while they were on vacation from the penitentiary.

Because of the circumstances in her community, Andrea often complained that all men were dogs, but really, she had fallen into the trap of thinking all men were the same because she was attracted to the same type of men. She looked for familiarity in a mate because it made her feel comfortable. She longed to be treated like the popular girl she was in high school because, in actuality, she had never really truly evolved. She never bothered looking outside her comfort zone, neighborhood, or community and wondered why she kept yielding the same results.

As we know, the unknown can be scary, especially when you are used to operating in a way where you pretty much know what to expect. Because her past experiences taught her to keep her expectations low, she condemned herself to a lifetime of singleness or on-and-off-again relationships. Staying in one's comfort zone is a mistake too many of us make. Sometimes we are easily turned off by men that we say are not "our type," but get mistreated by the ones who are. A type should have more to do with your basic level of compatibility, his character and his ambition than his swag, reputation, pockets, or familiarity.

Some believe that the bar has been set so low that women accept less than what they deserve merely because they have very little to choose from. At this point, I want you to intentionally and strategically add to your well-thought-out life plan and ensure you're not wasting time dating men who are not on your level.

Keep in mind that you will most likely need to venture outside of your comfort zone, which may mean dating outside of your hometown, state, and as a last result your "race". In case you are still wondering, did I mean to say your "level" earlier? Why yes, yes, I did! You may be one of those very accomplished women who really has her shit together and understands that the odds are severely stacked against the Black male in this country. Many of us grew up witnessing our male family members and friends being targeted by the police, experiencing racism on the job, locked up in prisons for decades for petty crimes, or many other injustices we experience in our everyday lives. But at some point, a spade is still a spade.

Yes, all of these things affect how we view the males in our communities and how we want to protect and love them. Black women have always been willing to embrace a man down on his luck because we saw potential, but our real hope was that these men would love, appreciate, and choose us in return. Most men, on the other hand, usually do not operate that way. It is no secret that our men, no matter their own economic status, will seek out the highest quality Black woman because there is always a chance that she will oblige, simply because there are not enough eligible Black men to choose from.

Before you go out and become, or continue to be, a Captain Save a Hoe, consider this: **a man who has nothing to lose will make you lose everything!** When dealing with a man of a lower caliber, you must first understand that sometimes it is his own fault. Yes, there are exceptions to these rules, including systemic racism, mass incarceration, and increasing unemployment. But for the most part, we can choose the type of person we want to be, and curate the type of life we want. It just takes strategy, time, hard work, and planning. Often, the type of men you decide to spend your time with can come down to a matter of life and death, so choose wisely.

Gaining and Recognizing Your Power!

In order to balance out the power dynamics and reduce dating fatigue within our communities, you may need to reduce your visibility and access from potential mates. This means not going out with men you know you are not attracted to or who you feel do not meet your basic standards or requirements. By being very careful who you spend your time with, you are limiting the poor-quality experiences that can be had with a man you know you did not want in the first place.

I believe some of the ways to gain power are simply by making yourself more valuable, unique, and not so easy to access. Men know that "dateable" women are abundant in their cities and on dating apps, but there is not a myriad of compatible matches. A date with a beautiful Black woman is usually just a swipe away, but what qualities, talents, and skills set you apart? My theory is that by making yourself the prize from inception, you immediately hold the majority of the cards. This process is for those who are serious about dating and who are dating with intention. This is not for those willing to go out with anyone without a plan to see where it goes. As we continue in this chapter, remember that this "game plan" is for austere players only.

First, before meeting with your potential mate, he should put in some work just to have the luxury of a conversation or date with you. You are not one of the options on the fast-food menu, also known as a dating app. You are not willing to put yourself in an apple barrel for any man who thinks you are attractive to bob for. You immediately become a goal, whether it be short-lived or long-term. You are telling the male that you are worth this extra step, and he has to work to get your attention. Men love a challenge, and as I have mentioned before, men value the things they have to work for the most.

My personal way of doing this was by creating a custom compatibility form (visit the website www.pimpettechronicles.com for example) that suitors had to fill out before talking to me. Since I am a busy, secure woman who enjoys her alone time and does not mind being single, you (the man) must first show me that you are worth even giving you a moment of my time. Being single for me has never equated to being lonely. Since men love to jump into our inboxes via social media, when they'd ask me if I was single, I simply responded yes, and told them that I was accepting applications. They immediately think I am joking, and that is when I send them the custom form I created, which includes a series of questions that help determine compatibility. Most men are eager to fill it out because they are naturally competitive, and very few men have refused thus far.

When refused, this told me they were most likely the type who would feel that they were the prize and that I would compete with other women for their attention. The refusal meant, how dare I, a woman, ask him to prove to me that he is worthy of my attention? They immediately let me know they were aware and secure with the assertion that the women-to-man ratio was in their favor and I should be working to make him want me. I have zero interest in competing for something I probably don't even want. I only have time to get to know men who meet my very basic requirements. The first and most important requirement is his ability to show me that he wants to get to know Tinisha, not that he is just looking for any woman to pass the time with.

This form was to be completed by him and then assessed by me, all before I would even agree to have a real conversation with him. It is then scored with the max points being 200 and the minimum being 150 points to be eligible to have a conversation with me. Occasionally, some men would ask me to fill out one in return. I would simply call their bluff and tell them to send me a custom form designed by them, and I would complete it. This is to just make them feel that they have a little bit of power in the situation. To date, none of them have sent me a damn thing.

I declined to have a conversation first because I have found that many of the conversations, whether good or bad, usually lead to nowhere. In the past, men I met virtually and talked to from dating sites were often lonely and needed a therapist as opposed to a mate. At some point during the dating app stage in my life, I started to feel like I should charge for my online counseling services. Like, who the fuck am I, Dr. Phil? After those conversations, the players would realize that getting to me was going to require some work, and since most men are used to some modern women being easy and in a hurry to run off on a date with them. While men are typically lazy these days, very few would actively pursue me, but most wanted to remain connected via social media. I still often have great conversations on Fakebook with the men I never dated from the dating apps. Hey, y'all!

Now, I know a pre-date application (that I prefer to call a compatibility form) may seem unconventional, but I refuse to allow myself to be treated like an option in all my grace and wisdom. Since I have placed myself in a position of power (I can take care of myself completely), I am free to be as picky and selective as I desire. Know your own value and then decide what is advantageous for you.

Maybe you want a softer approach that includes a conversation and then easing in a form. Perhaps you don't want to use this method at all. I am only sharing what has worked for me thus far, and there is no shortage of would-be suitors in my life. I do quite well. Since men usually approach women, my thought is, why should we have to jump through hoops to prove to him we are worthy? If you are to approach the man, then you are putting yourself in the position of having to prove your worthiness. I am not saying that it may not work sometimes, but I am not about that life.

To further explain how the form works, we would only move to the conversation stage if the man scored over 150 points. This is where you actually pick up the phone and talk to the person. I know this may sound foreign to some younger folk, but back in my day, we wanted to hear how a fella sounded before we agreed to meet up with him. It has been my experience that the best way to miscommunicate these days is via text message. Way to go, technology.

So now that I already know that he mostly matches on paper and meets my most basic requirements, which include sexual ones, let's see if he can hold his own on the phone. If the conversation goes well, you move forward with the first date or meeting. It could be something as simple as having a coffee in the afternoon, or if you both really are feeling each other, you can sit down for a meal. From here, the rest is up to the man. Dear fellas, if the woman has agreed to meet you in person, she is saying that you are interesting enough to "consider" having sex with. On that first date, you can either talk yourself out of her drawers or move a step closer to getting into them. The choice is yours.

To continue, the first date is what I consider the most important because this is when your energy meets his energy. Your souls may like each other or be in complete conflict. Sometimes you just don't move well together. Maybe it's the way he walks or the way he chews his food. Regardless of the reason, the first date, or at most the second, will inevitably tell you whether or not you want to date this person. If they come off as someone you don't want to spend time with, you simply do not move forward. It does not take more than a couple of dates to see if you wish to be pursued or not. I will only go on one date, and if it goes well, he is in the running. If not, I will let him know I am not interested.

When people were asked what they would do if someone asked them to fill out a custom dating form, surprisingly, the majority of men thought it was a great idea because it gave the person an indication of what they may be getting into ahead of time. They also felt it would eliminate a bunch of games or uncomfortable situations later down the line. Below are some of the responses from a survey completed when the question was raised about whether or not they would fill out a custom compatibility form. Most participants were considered to be seriously seeking a mate and were over the age of 30.

1. Kay (Female, 43): "I'm here for it! Let's not waste time!"

2. A.M. (Female, 45): "Why not? It's a 50/50 chance either way."

3. Bob (Male, 63): "I would try it out of curiosity."

4. Phe (Female, 44): "I would fill it out. Much better to get the compatibility out the way. Gives us more to talk about on the first date. If I fail the questionnaire and there is no first date, then that's cool, too."

5. Adr (Female, 45): "Like, a survey that I have to answer questions? I'd pass on that person because they would strike me as either liking to be in control or maybe they have had too many failures, not healed from relationships, or too guarded. That person would find these things out fairly early via a few phone calls and after an outing or two. I don't like

to waste folks' time or have mine wasted, but honestly, a questionnaire seems disingenuous."

6. Michale (Male, 57): "I've been suggesting this to my friends for years!"

7. Tee (Female, 35): "I honestly would rather spend 10 minutes filling out a series of questions than being forced to sit in front of them, get to know them, then determine that we have little to nothing in common, or that the basic things I require or desire in a relationship, they do not possess. I don't like wasting time or spending time with men I see no future in."

8. Kat (Female, 65): "A questionnaire? Seriously? Have we sunk to the point that we can't be bothered to take the time for human interaction even if it doesn't work out?"

9. Brenda (Female, 34): "Never. In fact, I would cross him off the list for future dates."

10. Corn (Male, 46): "I would be intrigued and sorry that I did not think of it first!"

11. Dave (Male, 48): "Seems like that would take a little something out of the first date. Questionnaire request... Red flag for me."

12. Olive (Female, 63): "I would be intrigued by this person because they don't want to waste time on the wrong person.

It's all about compatibility. Some couples struggle through their pre-marital counseling sessions because they haven't discussed many issues brought to their attention in compatibility questionnaires. Even dating sites like Match use compatibility questionnaires."

13. GB (Male, 65): "Seriously, it allows easy communication to a great understanding and true love for serious-minded people, not just fulfilling occasional concerns for temporary, blinded love affairs."

14. MaryAnn (Female, 42): "Honestly, now that I am older, I think it is a great idea."

15. Reese Pooh (Male, 60): "I would not do it unless it was someone I really wanted, bad."

16. Denisqa (Female, 40): "Never! In fact, I would cross him off the list of potential future dates."

17. Mal (Male, 32): "Yes, I would do it!"

18. Jay (Male, 53): "I wouldn't mind. Would be interested to read each other's and discuss our answers."

19. Allana (Female, 49): "I love it! Finding compatible prospects prescreened is far more efficient."

20. Stephon (Male, 30): "It is a good idea in principle, but it may be difficult in practice."

21. Wizard Khalifa (Male, 50): "I think it's a good idea, but some guys may be offended by it."

22. Efesk (Male, 62): "Definitely! I promise a lot of men wouldn't get hired. Been suggested this for about 20 years

Out of the 22 people surveyed, seven women said yes, and four said no. Amongst the men, nine men thought it was a great idea, and only two said no. When further questioned, most men understood that it would, in the long run, save them money (because they were less likely to be dating someone who just wanted a free meal), and they would immediately know that this woman meant business and not to waste her time.

They understood that she was most likely not looking to just date anyone, and the men would feel special if chosen. My question is, why wouldn't he? The survey also proved that most serious-minded people are tired of the merry-go-round of dating and are looking for a way to only date those they are compatible with, at least on paper.

How Serious Are You?

If you are a woman who lives in the Midwest like me, finding that quality single Black man can sometimes seem challenging. Social media makes it appear like everyone has one except you. In a virtual world so big, just exactly where should you start? Well, since you paid good money for this book, I thought it would be my duty to try and help a sista out.

Below are the stats from Blackdemographics.com[3] that show the numbers for FULL TIME working Black men in these cities per 100 Black women. This does not specify whether or not the men are single, but at least we have an idea of where we may have to consider taking a little road trip!

FULL TIME - WORKING POPULATIONS OF 50,000 OR MORE		MEDIAN HOUSING INCOME 2020 PER CENSUS
SAN DIEGO, CA	167 Black MEN / 100 Black WOMEN	MEDIAN HOUSEHOLD INCOME $83, 454 PER CAPITA INCOME $43,090
SEATTLE, WA	139 Black MEN / 100 Black WOMEN	MEDIAN HOUSEHOLD INCOME $97,185 PER CAPITA INCOME $63,610
DENVER, CO	134 Black MEN/ 100 Black WOMEN	MEDIAN HOUSEHOLD INCOME $72,661 PER CAPITA INCOME $45,636
PHOENIX, AZ	121 Black MEN/ 100 Black WOMEN	MEDIAN HOUSEHOLD INCOME $60,914 PER CAPITA INCOME $31,427
MINNEAPOLIS-ST PAUL, MN	120 Black MEN/ 100 Black WOMEN	MEDIAN HOUSEHOLD INCOME $66,068

[3] https://blackdemographics.com/population/black-male-statistics/

		PER CAPITA INCOME $40,368

FULL TIME - WORKING POPULATIONS OF 15,000 - 50,000		MEDIAN HOUSING INCOME 2020 PER CENSUS
PORTLAND, OR-WA	151 Black MEN / 100 Black WOMEN	MEDIAN HOUSEHOLD INCOME $39,538 PER CAPITA INCOME $21,786
CLARKSVILLE, TN- KY	138 Black MEN / 100 Black WOMEN	MEDIAN HOUSEHOLD INCOME $55,819 PER CAPITA INCOME $26,312
SAN JOSE- SANTA CLARA, CA	131 Black MEN / 100 Black WOMEN	MEDIAN HOUSEHOLD INCOME $117,324 PER CAPITA INCOME $49,207
PROVIDENCE, RI - MA	130 Black MEN / 100 Black WOMEN	MEDIAN HOUSEHOLD INCOME $49,065 PER CAPITA INCOME $28,733
KILLEEN - TEMPLE, TX	129 Black MEN / 100 Black WOMEN	MEDIAN HOUSEHOLD INCOME $50,335 PER CAPITA INCOME $23,871

FULL TIME - WORKING POPULATIONS OF 5,000 - 15, 000		MEDIAN HOUSING INCOME 2020 PER CENSUS
URBAN HONOLULU, HI	294 Black MEN/100 Black WOMEN	MEDIAN HOUSEHOLD INCOME $72,454 PER CAPITA INCOME $39,235
EL PASO, TX	195 Black MEN / 100	MEDIAN HOUSEHOLD INCOME

	Black WOMEN	$48,866 PER CAPITA INCOME $23,450
SALT LAKE CITY, UT	180 Black MEN / 100 Black WOMEN	MEDIAN HOUSEHOLD INCOME $63,156 PER CAPITA INCOME $39,126
OXNARD-VENTURA, CA	163 Black MEN/ 100 Black WOMEN	MEDIAN HOUSEHOLD INCOME $77,050 PER CAPITA INCOME $24,688
ALBUQUERQUE, NM	162 Black MEN / 100 Black WOMEN	MEDIAN HOUSEHOLD INCOME $53,936 PER CAPITA INCOME $31,103

Looking at these cities and states, one can't help but notice that only one place, Minnesota, is in the Midwest. Just think, the first mass migration in the states for Black folks was when our grand- or great-grandparents started fleeing the South to the North to escape racism and the horrors that came along with it. Now, it appears that some of us Northern women may have to do a little migrating ourselves, just so that we can have a better chance at finding a mate who looks like us! This may be even more important to women of childbearing age.

When mentioning this concept of relocating to one millennial woman who was whining about being unable to find a mate, she referred to the concept of being "in search of dick." This let me know immediately that this poor, unfortunate being had never known the value of a good man. When a woman has a good man in her corner, she too can move mountains. Contrary to what some may say, a man's value is not just determined by his dick or his wallet. Having a compatible mate is invaluable, and if you need to relocate to get yours, please don't hesitate to do so. *P.S., please make sure you do it wisely and have a plan in place first. Job, housing, etc.*

When All Else Fails?

I sometimes hear women say that men do not know how to court them anymore. My response is, "Who are y'all dating?" Even at a time when the Black-men-to-Black-women ratio is higher than that of his female counterpart, as is the case in all ethnic groups, according to the World Population Review[4], if you are strategic and have made yourself an asset and not a liability, you can still manage to date men who are willing to take you out and treat you like a lady.

There is this fear being circulated that has Black women believing that the racial disparity between the sexes is a lot worse than what it may truly be, which benefits none other than the male. My thought is, if it is true (which I cannot confirm or deny after many attempts to find a definitive answer), then make certain that you, too, are considered a unicorn amongst horses, which goes back to **being the best version of you**. As a woman, it is your duty to ensure that you are treated well in all regards. Never move in desperation, even if you

---

4https://worldpopulationreview.com/state-rankings/male-to-female-ratio-by-state

are in a room full of 100 women and 10 men. What is for you will be for you.

I recently spoke to an older single lady who has her act together in every aspect of the term, and she said that the competition was rough out there. My thought again is, why would you ever want to compete with another woman? If he came to you, approached you, and asked to get to know you, then why should you have to prove yourself worthy of him, especially in comparison to another woman?

For example, does that employer fill out a job application for you if you apply for a job? Absolutely not! So, in dating and courting, it is the man who should be proving his worthiness since he is in pursuit of you. If I make myself available to him for a date, I am allowing him the opportunity to get to know me. At that stage, he may decide that he does not want the job after all, which is absolutely within his right. His task is to prove himself worthy of my time, and mine is simply to show him what he may get for all his efforts. On the flip side, I might learn that he does not fit my requirements, or he may find the job entirely too hard. Some women require more work than others, and that's cool, too. Stay in your own lane, brotha! The point I am making is, since women generally do not approach men, then why would women need to prove themselves worthy of a man's advances?

As mentioned many times before (because I don't want y'all to forget), the Black Man has an excess of women to choose from. In all actuality, they have the freedom to date outside their race with very little pushback from the community or anyone, which is why they are twice as likely to intermarry compared to Black women.[5]

For those Black women who are brave enough to do so, they are labeled as sellouts, bed wenches, coons, etc. Admittingly, at one time, I too, felt that it was wrong for a Black person to date outside their race, but the more I've dated and found it ever so challenging to find a commitment-minded Black man, the more I started to change my viewpoint.

I totally get the "we were together on the slave ships, and we have been holding each other down for 400 years" thought process behind Black women exclusively being with Black men. But I became open to the possibility after seeing how slim the choices have become in my community and, statistically, of finding a suitable Black male who is: A) not trying to get you to jump through hoops; B) sharing him with other women; C) making you compete with other women; or my favorite in most recent days, D) make him feel pretty.

At the time, the goal was simply to put myself in a position to have more choices, and fortunately, it worked out in my favor. Even though in that relationship we grew apart, I was never treated like an option. I learned from that experience just how well a working-class,

[5] Pew Research Center
https://www.pewresearch.org/social-trends/2017/05/18/1-trends-and-patterns-in-intermarriage/

middle-income man "could" treat his woman if he wanted to. Now, I demand nothing but the same or better from anyone I choose to spend my time with. After all, who wouldn't strive to be treated as well, or even greater, than they were in the past? Would you willingly turn in a new car for a used one? In all stages of life, the goal should be to upgrade!

If Black women are growing tired of fishing in this small pond of eligible Black males, who could really judge? I've been back in these dating streets for a couple of years now, and I must say that things have drastically changed, but let's take a moment to acknowledge it is not just in the Black community. White women are having similar problems, yet the issues they have are not as complex, nor my business.

If we throw mass incarceration, white supremacy, under- and unemployment, self-hate, colonization, police brutality, and basically everything associated with a group of displaced people into the mix, then we can see how serious our problem is in comparison. The challenge is further complicated because "we" Black women limit ourselves to who we date based on race/ethnicity, often in spaces where the numbers are not in our favor.

Let's be clear. I firmly believe in people loving and being with whomever, they want, regardless of ethnic group, gender, sex, etc. And, in case you weren't aware, according to Population Reference

Bureau[6], most Americans prefer to marry within their own "race," and with Black women, that is no exception. I honestly suspect that most Black women only choose to date outside of their "race" (which I believe does not exist, but that's a different conversation) as a last resort or because that is what's available to them. I know this to be true in my own personal experience.

So, the next time one looks at a single Black woman and criticizes her for dating outside of her group, please instead refer her to the next eligible Black male that you know personally has good character and his shit together. I asked a married male friend of mine once to do that, and he could not name one single friend that he felt would make a suitable life partner. He instead just shook his head and said the brothas nowadays were fucked up.

Getting back to the issue, according to the National Center for Education Statistics[7], Black women are now the most educated group in the United States. As a result, we have now become the least likely to marry. Somebody got some 'splainin' to do (in my Ricky Ricardo voice). The reason, I suspect, is simply because people with a higher socioeconomic status (which comes with education) usually seek a partner in the same category. Marrying and dating a man outside of your own socioeconomic status, or for our purposes, we will say "level," is usually avoided for good reason.

---

[6] https://www.prb.org/resources/most-americans-marry-within-their-race/
[7] https://nces.ed.gov/fastfacts/display.asp?id=72

Generally speaking, people who come from or live in environments where struggle is the norm are not so eager to return to it once a relationship that equates to a "come up" is over. Try providing a potential mate with something that he may not be accustomed to, such as a fancy home, plentiful food, expensive clothes, etc., and then try to strip it away. If the person is mentally stable, then he may just walk away, but if not, the breakup will not be smooth. Remember, living in a stressful economic environment means that, more than ever, people are likely to be dealing with mental illness. This is another reason why I believe it is important that you only date men who are generally happy in their own life.

So why is it that our average Black men are failing to realize what they have at their disposal and are creating an environment that ultimately makes the woman have to choose her own happiness and survival over Black solidarity? Let's also note that even when a Black woman chooses to date a Black male with a lower educational and economic status than her, she will often be met with distrust or the competition of the notorious side chick. It would seem that a brotha (especially those on the lower economic tier than their mate) who manages to get a woman with her act together would do everything in his power to keep her. But in all of his arrogance and big dick energy (whether real or exaggerated), he will most likely keep up with the inconsistencies, game, and/or promiscuity. When called out, some may not walk away easily.

In addition, "Good" Black men are starting to recognize that many of the men in our communities are simply jealous of the women, and those toxic dudes are obsessed with trying to humble those of us who excel. What better way to humble a woman than to pit her against other women or make her compete for you, the man, who most likely has less going for himself than she does? I hope that some of these good men would start doing something to change this dysfunctional behavior, such as offering a little guidance to the ones who are failing in the character department or the brothas who are contributing to the broken hearts and broken homes epidemic.

We become part of the problem when we stand by and allow disrespect. When you sit around and chat it up with dudes who aren't being responsible, then you are supporting the damage they are causing. How often have we witnessed a man intentionally trying to bring a woman down a peg? The self-hate is real, and I see no end to these issues anytime soon. They are complex, and although most can agree that it is by design, like so many other issues amongst the Black community, no one can agree on how to remediate them.

On another note, be wary of men who think they have a little bit of wealth, who act suspicious, cheap, and petty while courting you. Even if you never ask him for a thing, he will be looking for some sign that you are after his imaginary pot of gold. If you should ever dare to request any assistance, he will immediately believe that you are a gold digger. My rule is that if I must ask, then I do not want it. Please note that if a man is willing to watch you struggle in any regard and does not offer to assist, he does not have your best interest at heart, and it is best to move on and cut your losses. You should not have to prove yourself to anyone, especially one who asked to come into your world. Sometimes the man making $60,000 per year will care for you better than the one making $120,000. If he does not see your overall value and net worth, he does not deserve you anyway.

Recently, a well-known radio host made an interesting statement where he mentioned the white male's goal was always to have the Black woman by his side. He further stated that the way to have the Black woman by his side was to eliminate the Black male as competition. He concluded that this has, in fact, mostly been accomplished via the help of mass incarceration. I agree with him to an extent, but honestly, it is starting to look more like Black men are eliminating themselves, mostly by continuously playing games with the women they date and simply devaluing the Black woman as a whole.

We see it every time a Black man gains a little success and immediately chooses to marry outside his own ethnic group. It is often his belief (and a myth) that in doing so, he is upgrading from the type of woman he most likely used to help get him where he has arrived. The good ole Black woman.

The greatest, most recent example could be seen where a Black billionaire uplifted an entire non-Black family, making his wife with zero talent a billionaire, to eventually have her leave him for a white man, conveniently, after birthing four kids by him. Cha-ching!

This billionaire (aka knucklehead) admitted to giving her "Black Culture" and even bragged about it. We can conclude that he felt marrying a non-Black woman would be an upgrade because he implied such in his song (y'all know the one). Had he married a Black woman, can you imagine how this type of wealth could have affected her entire family and the community? But in the end, the success rate for that interracial couple (and others) continues to be no greater than had he just married within his own ethnic group. Statistically, he had a better chance of success had he chosen a Black woman, and let me just add that even when white men marry Black women, they also have a better success rate. Things that make ya go, hmm.

I hope that the brothers wake up quickly because they are coming for your beautiful, often curvaceous, golden, caramel-to-chocolate-dipped women. If you have a Black woman, treat her right and stop playing because the competition for quality Black women is about to get fierce! Black women are starting to date and intermarry for the first time since being in this country. It has often been said that one may love a good old steak every now and then, but a hamburger ain't bad either. Or, in case you didn't catch that, what I used to say to my favorite ex was, "I may love your ass, but a substitute is just fine." Strong women **WILL** eventually walk away from any love that is causing them pain, even if it is Black Love.

Ultimately, my overall advice to anyone is to be with whoever treats you the best because, truthfully, we only have one life to live, and at some point, you have to choose your own happiness. One thing I will add for those who decide to venture outside the Black zone, please make sure that if you do it, you do it well! Brad better be treating your ass like a queen, or don't even waste your time. If you need an example of someone who did it quite well, that would be Eve.

And please remember, all men can cause you pain, and all relationships will have problems. Every man should be vetted and met with the same caution regardless of his ethnicity. Actually, I will even go as far as to say more! The last thing you want to find out is that you are being fetishized or that he is a closet racist. Just know that if you venture to the other side, make sure that you are being treated **superbly, and if you ever find yourself competing with another woman or in any bullshit**, start over and throw that fish back in the pond.

Single Mothers Only

Being single can be extremely challenging for mothers, and sometimes it can get a little lonely. The majority of my dating years were spent as a young mother with two children. I have also spent most of those years in long-term, monogamous relationships. My close friends used to tease me and say that I monkey bar through men. The few that were around when my daughters were growing up lasted for about six years each. These men met me and then wanted to jump into a relationship, which is why I have been engaged several times. Luckily, the marriages never happened, but the choice to marry or not has always been mine. That is a story for another book.

Now that I am as seasoned as a good ole piece of fried buttermilk chicken, and my girls are adults completely on their own, I no longer move with the concerns that I had as a young, single mother with two daughters, and I take my time when choosing a mate. When you have children, you have to navigate through life in an entirely different way. You must constantly be on the lookout for predators and be cautious about who you bring around your children, man or woman. You must be extra careful who you date because you want to make sure you are around to raise your babies. You do not have the luxury of hanging with drug dealers, criminals, or any other low-level dudes.

When my children were young, I would first analyze the potential to see if he would be good for my children and me. I chose who would be the most beneficial to our lives as a whole. It didn't matter how cute or sexy he was if I found him to be selfish or completely uninterested in my well-being or that of my girls.

I chose those who understood the assignment and made it clear that they wanted to be a part of my world, which included all extensions of me. I slowly introduced them to my daughters, and I only dated men who had daughters of their own. This was because I believed men who held healthy relationships with their daughters were least likely to be predators. I further believed that if I could reduce the likelihood in any regard, I definitely would. Thankfully, in my situation, my analysis was right.

In my lifetime, I have been blessed to have met really good men who still, to this day, my daughters and I can call on in the case of an emergency. I have learned that there are good men in the world, but that does not necessarily mean that they are a good fit for you. I believe someone can be good to you but not necessarily your match.

As mothers, our first obligation is to ensure our children are provided for, protected, and loved. If the man couldn't make life better for the family I built, then he was not an option. Yes, as a woman, I understand that you want to feel loved and all that jazz, but once you bring someone else into this world, your needs and wants are secondary. Please trust me when I say, if a man is truly into you, he will make sure that you and your babies are taken care of and never take anything away from your child. That includes all your time.

This does not mean that he will not want or deserve alone time with you, but a good mate will only feel comfortable doing so once he knows your kids are being taken care of. This also doesn't mean that he is now responsible for what you and your children's father should be responsible for (which is your kids), just that he will more than likely desire to pick up where the other man falls short or simply add extra.

Also, remember that men will judge you based on how you prioritize them in the relationship. If you are willing to drop everything on a whim to have fun with him, he will most likely not take you seriously and believe you are a bad parent overall. Especially if, someday, he wants children of his own.

The fact is that grown men understand that to date a woman with a child, he is getting a packaged deal, and any man coming into your life should not be hesitant, alarmed, or act jealous when you have to divide your time between him and your offspring. The really good men will show you that they want to care for you and your children. They will eventually encourage you to sometimes bring them along on your dates.

Too often, we hear stories about boyfriends and husbands that are not the kids' natural father (and sometimes even the father) doing something horrible to the child, and we wonder how the mother did not see the signs. My advice is to always be extra careful who you bring around and teach your children to tell you everything. Also, teach them to yell and say no to people who touch them or make them feel uncomfortable. A child who is empowered to speak will grow up to be a powerful human being.

The key is to remain alert and never let your guard down. Always be proactive in protecting your children, and never ignore the signs that tell you something is off. If you get a gut feeling about something, you are most likely right. Your child is your most valuable asset, and their protection is more important than your gratification. Be mindful of who you are dating and really get to know them before letting them completely into your world.

Nipping it in the Bud!

Tina was a young single mother of two school-aged girls. She had been single for a couple of years after being in an abusive relationship with her children's father. She was living in an apartment building next door to her good friend Leslie, who always mentioned how Tina should find a man to help take care of her and her girls. Tina was in no hurry to settle down again and was comfortable with the quiet life she had built with her children. She kept a neat, clean apartment and worked full-time to provide for her family. She was living paycheck-to-paycheck, but overall, their basic needs and some of their wants were met.

One day, Leslie asked Tina if she could introduce her to Ron, a friend of a man she was dating. She told Tina he was a nice-looking, slightly-older gentleman who worked at Chrysler. Leslie was impressed that Ron drove a fancy sports car and had no children. She said they were stopping by that night and would bring some drinks.

Tina hesitantly agreed. Leslie was older and more experienced than she was, so Tina looked up to her and often took her advice. If she thought Ron was a good catch, then he must be.

Soon, Leslie, Ron, and Joe, Leslie's boo, were at Tina's door. Tina was thrown off because she had assumed that they all would just chill outside of the apartment on the picnic tables like she and Leslie usually did. Tina reluctantly let them in. Immediately, Ron walked into her apartment, strutting like a peacock. In a big hefty voice, he looked at Tina and said, "Mm, mm, mm, I like what I see." Tina was immediately turned off by Ron. Tina despised men who sized her up and thought she needed their approval.

Ron began strutting around her apartment and saying how nice it was. He even went as far as to confidently look into the bedrooms and exclaimed, "Oh, this would work out nice!" Seeing how uncomfortable Tina appeared, Leslie tried to rectify the situation by properly introducing them. Tina looked at Leslie and gave her a look that said, "What the fuck is this?" Ron had not even spoken two sentences to Tina and was already trying to figure out how he could move into her place. Tina was young but not dumb.

It was a late-summer afternoon, and Tina's children were playing in the yard with the other kids in the neighborhood. She sat near the window where she could see and talk to them. She was already certain that Ron was not a match, and she was irritated that Leslie had brought such a clown to meet her. No amount of money, nor fancy car, was worth her ever giving up her **POWER** to be led by a man who didn't even know how to get his foot in the door before assuming that she would want him. He was totally uncouth and clearly used to getting what he wanted from women. He was a very handsome, tall, cocoa-brown man, but all she saw was an arrogant headache. She was not interested.

As the evening went on, they all talked and laughed while Tina sat waiting for it to be over. During the conversation, she brought up the fact that she held her CPL and that her brother stayed with her periodically, just in case Ron's ass was some psycho. She did not want him to know that it was just her and her two daughters living there. If he was a lunatic, she wanted to make it known to him that she was not gonna be an easy target or victim. She was mad at herself and Leslie for having to think like this. She realized that Leslie was not as wise as she thought she was.

After a while, Tina leaned out the window and called out to her daughters that they would have to come in for bed in 15 minutes. As time passed, Ron kept looking out of the window and looking at his watch. Soon, it was time for the girls to come in. Ron quickly yelled out the window to Tina's children, "Y'all come on in now; it's time to come in." Tina was horrified, and Leslie saw it on her face and began to laugh uncomfortably. Tina looked out the window at her kids, who looked shocked and scared, partly because they had not even met this random dude and because a stranger was making demands and shouting at them. At that moment, Tina knew he had her fucked up.

She then told everyone that it was time for her to put her kids in the tub, and she turned to Ron and politely said, "It was nice meeting you." Leslie and her dynamic duo left, and Tina began to get her children ready for bed. She was disappointed in herself for allowing this to happen.

The next day, Ron called Tina, said he had a nice time, and asked when he could see her again. Tina firmly said that she was not interested and that she was getting back with the kids' father (a lie nonetheless). He asked her why she agreed to meet him, and she simply said that she was not sure until this morning. Luckily, Ron bowed out gracefully and never called her again. This was a life lesson for Tina because this situation could have gone bad for many reasons. Her biggest lesson was to never allow anyone, no matter who they were, to bring random dudes to her house and to not follow behind Leslie blindly. Older ain't always wiser.

What Tina did right was read those red flags. The first one was when Ron made reference to his approval of her in a way that suggested the choice was completely up to him. Nowadays, men who still look at women as if they are standing on the auction block are the kind you want to stay clear of. The second was when Ron felt comfortable enough to strut around a woman's home, someone he just met, and reference how comfortable it would be for him. And the final and biggest one was when he had the audacity, to yell at her kids and order them to do anything.

In Tina's mind, if he was this comfortable on the first day of meeting her, without even having any type of relationship with her or her daughters, what else would he be potentially comfortable to do? Her instincts were to protect her most valuable asset at any cost, which meant turning down a potential "catch" if he exhibited any controlling or questionable behaviors. A grown man who would order someone else's little girls around so easily gave an indication of what type of relationships he has been in and what type of power he held in them.

Men in my life have often told me that they personally would not even trust some of their male friends, who were daughterless, around their own daughters. We know that all men aren't predators, but unfortunately, the ones who are, do not wear a sign telling us. So, until they prove otherwise, our guards should always be up. Childhood is a short part of life and should be spent happily and trauma-free. The ultimate job of a mother is to protect her offspring.

Don't Be Fooled by the Oakie Doke!

As a single mother, you may sometimes run into a special breed of Kneegrow who will prey on you. These clowns are the kind of dudes who intentionally go after women with children to simply string along. They are looking to settle down with a woman without children, but meanwhile, they will fuck and date the ones who have them, unbeknownst to her of his true nature. Sadly, these types are the hardest to decode because "slick" is their middle name.

A couple of older friends of mine were strung along (on and off situationships) by the same two dudes for over a decade who later admitted they were simply waiting for these ladies' children to grow up before they would commit. They did not want to be a stepfather, and looking back, they actually showed signs of this all along.

Now that I am older and wiser, I can remember very few times, if any, when these clowns did anything to show that they cared about the children. I guess these women either ignored or did not see the red flags. Fate would have it; as these men grew old, they actually revealed this secret. By then, they were practically elderly, used up, and quite frankly, rather ugly. Nobody wanted them, not even the women they once had wrapped around their fingers. Remember, men, on average, do not hold up as well as women, so we'll always have that going for us. This is yet another reason why I say protect your beauty.

I personally knew of a man who had three kids he was half-ass raising and married a woman who had abandoned hers just so that they could run around, get drunk, and be irresponsible together. For men, it does not matter whether or not they themselves have children of their own; some single fathers still view a woman who has the responsibility to care for a child as less attractive than a woman who does not. The audacity!

These man-childs will start pretending to care about you and your babies but then start switching it up once they get the goods. I want you to always demand the best treatment, no matter how many children you have. If he switches up his energy, switch yours up, too. You will still make whoever is courting you continue to do the things we discussed in previous chapters and the things that you require him to do. Make sure he remains consistent.

Believe me when I say a grown ass man will recognize a good woman and mother, and he won't shy away from something as simple as a little responsibility. As long as you have that baby daddy in check (he is not a problem), and your shit is tight—meaning clean house, you look your best, you have your own money (enough to pay your bills, you don't have to be rich), can take care of you and your babies—you can still land a decent mate. He may even be a little older, but often, mature men make for excellent husbands to younger women. They are usually too old and tired to play games and generally just want peace. After all, men love to strut like a peacock, and what better way than having a chick a decade or more younger than him on his arm? In his eyes, he is immediately winning!

I can assure you that I have **NEVER** had a hard time finding a good man, even with two babies on my hip, because I have always carried myself in a way that demands respect, and men will fall at your feet when you do so. If he does not, kick his ass to the curb so hard that your ankles hurt. No time to be crying over spilled milk.

The reality is the more children you have, the harder it will be for you to find a suitable mate. But it is not impossible, so never let anyone make you feel that it is. My mother had four children before she married Husband Number Two, and my granny had seven when she found her second husband. Times have changed, but as long as you have made yourself **the best version of you,** you will still be considered a catch. But please, do not be out here birthing babies like you are trying to repopulate the earth. Children are expensive and should be brought into the world as long as you are certain YOU can provide for them. Momma's baby, Daddy's maybe.

As mentioned previously, keep in mind when deciding to have your children that since men are free to impregnate different women, many will move on to start an entirely new family with another chick with little regard for the ones they leave behind. Some will also impregnate multiple women just so that they can bounce between households throughout their lives. I don't know exactly what the science behind this is (definitely some bottom-feeder activity), but I have seen it entirely too often not to recognize it as a "thing." The only *thing* that will likely slow down a breeder is child support kicking his ass, and even then, some would rather hustle or work under the table than provide for their own offspring. #Goofy.

The bottom line is, ALWAYS, in all regards, ensure that you and yours are taken care of first and foremost. Just because you may already have a child does NOT mean you have to settle for anything less than what you desire. You can still have it all!

Chapter 6

Sex Life Matters

"Don't let nobody ruin your good time!"
Juanetta Hill, Auntie extraordinaire, circa 2019

We have all heard the saying, **"pussy has power,"** and maybe you believe it does or maybe not. For the sake of discussion, let's assume the aforementioned is fact and common knowledge. Let's review how this power can be used for good and not evil. The first thing we are going to address is the recent epidemic of POOR PUSSY MANAGEMENT, AKA P.P.M.

P.P.M. can be described as a woman using her pussy in a way that is not beneficial to her in the long run. These include but are not limited to the following:

1. Sex with someone who does not have your best interest a heart.

2. Sex with someone who does not respect you.

3. Sex with someone you see no future with and it doesn't benefit you in any form.

4. Sex with another woman's husband out of jealousy or spite.

5. Sex with another woman's man out of jealousy or spite.

6. Sex with a broke man where there are emotions involved.

7. Sex with someone who you cannot or do not want to be with, in a manner where you cannot have sex with the man you want to be with. For example, you can't bang your boyfriend because he may fall in since you've been banging Big Dick Ahmad all night.

8. Sex with a dude who will not take you out in public for whatever reason.

9. Sex with a dude who comes to your house with nothing but a dick in his hand.

10. Unprotected sex with a broke dude. What if you get pregnant?

11. Unprotected sex with a dude you know is fucking someone else and possibly multiple people.

12. Unprotected sex with a dude you are certain is cheating on you.

13. Unprotected sex with a dude who has done nothing to earn the pleasure of experiencing you in your entirety.

Notice that we did not include **"sex with a man who is married,"** simply because people have different rules about what is allowed in their marriage, and that ain't nobody's business but the persons involved. Since the purpose of this book is not to condemn, condone, nor scrutinize any woman who has gotten involved with a married man for whatever reason, the most to be said on the matter is, if you are going to, please make sure it benefits you and benefits you well.

That means that you should not have to want for anything, and if you find that you are, you are committing **poor pussy management**. Additionally, know that it is usually a dangerous game and people are not always honest about their relationships, so use your best judgment, be safe, and never get caught up.

You may also have recognized that the list does not include **"sex with a broke dude,"** as well. That is simply because there are levels to that shit. If he is so broke that he falls under our **hobo-sexual, homeless lover, or couch surfer** category mentioned in **Chapter 3,** he "may" be good for a roll in the hay every now and again, but do consider the safety guidelines previously mentioned, and operate with your own discretion under your own terms. Personally, I am too seasoned to waste my good pussy on a broke dude, but to each their own.

Sexual Compatibility

At some point in life, we all tend to get an idea of the things we enjoy in the bedroom and the things we do not. For many of us, while growing up, sex was shunned, which often led to the development of some unhealthy views of sexuality that many still struggle with to this day. Back in the day, the most that were said in my hood was that sex was nasty and smelly. My mother once described it as an act where some man was jumping up and down on you, putting slime all over you, and making your vagina stink. She described oral sex as something that only dick-sucking bitches did, and in no way did I want to be a dick-sucking bitch.

I was ill-equipped to really know how to approach sex confidently. After witnessing my older sister get pregnant on the first try, only to be rejected by the baby's father, I decided to get it over with at barely 16. What an awkward waste of time that was. This made me open season in some regard because I simply had no point of reference in terms of developing and discussing a sex life. Since those days, I have had my share of good and bad experiences, and at my age, I am confident in the things that I do and don't like.

If you grew up anything like me, no one told us that women could have orgasms, nor did they say that some of us could achieve three different types of climaxes: clitoral, vaginal, and anal. It was never mentioned that our bodies could ejaculate and that a true orgasm consists of vulva contractions that can be seen and felt by both parties. No one told us that one of the greatest pleasures in life is when you have one partner, and you and that person learn each other's body so well that you can cum at the same time with every encounter. Thank you, Mr. Boo.

Everything I had learned early on, including the smelly sex thing, turned out to be absolutely incorrect. It turns out that only occurs when the persons having sex don't wash their ass. When it comes down to compatibility, there have been lovers who fit like a glove and lovers who I would never allow to touch my body more than once. Since now I am not one who is interested in changing how I "perform," I seek mates who enjoy and require the same things that I do, and then together, we expand from that point. I learned through my encounters that, while one man was describing me as being rigid, another was describing me as a freak. One thought I encompassed nothing but feminine sexiness, and the other felt I was a little masculine and aggressive.

In actuality, their view of my skills and my sex appeal mattered very little to me, as I have long since come to the conclusion that I was responsible for my own sexual enjoyment and my perception of myself. In the end, it will sometimes come down to the other parties' previous experiences and their own sexual confidence. I am a firm believer in doing what gives you the maximum satisfaction, and **his** satisfaction comes secondary, not first. You are responsible for your own ecstasy and pleasure; if he happens to be there, that's good, too! But if not, oh well. Not saying be a selfish lover, but let him prove he is worthy before you pull them tricks out the bag.

So, just because his ex-wife, or even all (according to him, of course) of his previous women, enjoyed performing oral anilingus on him does not mean that you have to perform it. Or, if he is accustomed to entering an area that you consider "exit only," that doesn't mean you have to engage if you know that ain't your thing. These types of preferences and desires should be discussed very early on, and if you two cannot come to a mutual agreement on matters of the bedroom, then that may be grounds for severing the situationship. Never compromise yourself or compete with any woman in any form or fashion, especially in the bedroom.

Remember, there could be very specific reasons why you don't want or feel comfortable engaging in a particular sex act (or vice versa), and in no way should anyone ever be pressured to do so. One thing is for certain, good sex has never been the glue to keep a man, and there are too many women who have believed otherwise, living with regrets to this day.

Can You Guess His Dick Size or Nah?

It has often been said that size does not matter and that it is the motion of the ocean instead. Well, my thought is that it depends on the woman and what her sexual requirements are. Just as all penises come in different sizes, so do vulvas and vaginas. We rarely discuss the actual vagina in terms of size, and most basic men would describe them as just being tight or loose.

Some may not even understand that this magical part of a woman's body can expand and retract based on many factors, including age, level of arousal, and the number of births. The vagina can also become elongated and can best be characterized as an accordion that can go from four to eight inches in depth. The fact that some vaginas can become much deeper than others would explain why some women prefer shorter penises while others prefer longer ones.

Penis Length in Inches

Under 5 inches	Below Average
5.1 - 5.5 inches	Average
5.5 - 7.0 inches	Above Average
7.0 and above	Extremely Endowed

Of course, there are variances in preferences that include (but are not limited to) shape, girth, circumcised, uncircumcised, hooks, etc.

But at some point during a woman's sexual journey, she will learn (hopefully) what works best for her body and what does not. Once a woman figures that out, she will always wonder about a potential mate's genitalia in fear of his body parts not being compatible with hers, which is really all it comes down to when considering this most basic aspect of mating.

Many ways have been shared that will give insight into what you may be in for once meeting a potential mate's genitalia, and the scientific studies available online do not always coincide with the experiences of the women in our personal circles. For fun, let's go over some of the myths and beliefs experienced by the ladies in my own community and hometown. This info should not be taken literally, but just as a basis so that you can make a note and form your own assertion.

- **The Tall Skinny Guy (over 5'10):** When asked, most women stated that the tall skinny guys were often the most endowed men in their own personal sexual encounters.

- **The Big and Tall Guy (over 5'10):** When asked, most stated that these men usually had average to small size penises and that being a bigger man had nothing to do with the size of his penis.

- **The Slim to Regular Short Guy (under 5'9):** there was absolutely no correlation between the height of the man in comparison to penis size. Most interviewed said the short dudes were surprisingly well-endowed compared to the taller men they dated.

- **The Short Fat Guy (under 5'9):** The women interviewed would not admit to having had sex with anyone who fell into this category. They all said they were fearful and not inspired to have sex with a short man who could not see his penis if he looked down. No data available.

- **The Shoe Size:** According to science and the ladies in the community, there is no correlation between shoe size and penis length. Both parties agreed that shoe size gives no insight into the endowment of the man. Several women in the community added that many tall men who held what they considered large feet came up short in the penis category. Surprisingly, some short men with big or even small feet had above-average penises.

- **The Size of His Hands:** Some of those interviewed believed that the best way to determine if a man's size is suitable for you before you have sex was to check the size of his hands. Bigger hands often meant bigger penises, while smaller hands led to smaller penises. To a degree, as mentioned in the next paragraph, science also supports this hypothesis.

When examining the hands' theory, the best justification was found in an article from Men's Health Magazine[8], which stated, "According to the ***Asian Journal of Andrology***, having a shorter index finger compared to your ring finger could mean you have a bigger penis." Of course, there are always exceptions to the rule, but it appears that if size is in question, the hands or index finger would probably give you the most accurate insight.

Sexual Health

During the '80s, and the highlight of the AIDS epidemic, everywhere you looked, you would see a commercial or billboard encouraging people to practice safe sex. Nowadays, it has become more of an afterthought that school-aged children and young adults are seldom educated properly on. The CDC currently estimates that 1 in 5 people in the U.S. has a sexually transmitted infection[9]. Please note that this number only represents diagnosed and reported cases. Since most STIs are asymptomatic, many people are never diagnosed because they experience few to zero symptoms.

According to Jonathan Mermin, M.D., M.P.H., director of CDC's National Center for HIV/AIDS, Viral Hepatitis, STD, and TB Prevention, "At a time when STIs are at an all-time high, they have

---

[8]   https://www.menshealth.com/health/a38123633/index-finger-penis-size-ratio-tiktok/
[9] https://www.cdc.gov/nchhstp/newsroom/2021/2018-STI-incidence-prevalence-estimates.html

fallen out of the national conversation. Yet, STIs are a preventable and treatable national health threat with substantial personal and economic impact. There is an urgent need to reverse the trend of increasing STIs, especially in the wake of the COVID-19 pandemic, which has affected many STI prevention services."[10]

Adding the challenges that COVID-19 presented and the fact that many people do not go to see a doctor unless they have symptoms, there are still some STIs (such as herpes) that even a condom cannot guarantee to protect you from. In addition, condoms sometimes come off, are not used properly, break, or are not even present, whether both parties are in agreement or not. For example, it is not uncommon for a man to either slip a condom off during sex or not put one on at all without the knowledge of the other partner (FYI, THIS IS RAPE). Also, there are times when the condom can be, in a sense, vacuumed off by the vagina without the woman knowing, with the man failing to tell her because it felt too good to stop, or he did not notice himself.

With all of these variables, it would only seem wise that you strive to only share one of your most valuable assets with those who you feel are truly worthy. The fact remains that every time we share our bodies, we are potentially putting ourselves in harm's way. Many people living with an STI simply will not share this info with a

---

[10]   https://www.cdc.gov/media/releases/2021/p0125-sexualy-transmitted-infection.html

potential partner or have no clue. In my opinion, it is best practice to assume that everyone has some sort of STI until proven otherwise. For maximum safety, the CDC recommends yearly testing and testing after each sexual partner.

Yes, I know this is another one of those subjects commonly left out of the dating conversation, but it should be at the top of the list. The reality is that you or someone close to you will have become exposed to an STI at some point. In the past, we were taught that it was always that person's fault or that it only happens to those who are careless and/or reckless. After working in a sexually transmitted disease clinic during Covid, hearing stories, and meeting people, I have been enlightened. I've learned of healthy relationships where one of the partners was HIV positive, and the other was not. There are also many cases where one partner was diagnosed with Herpes Simplex Virus 2, and the other partner did not contract it, even after being married for decades since the diagnosis.

My question to you is, since we know the probability is so high that you have had or know someone living with an STI, how do you think you'd react if you were to meet a potential mate who disclosed their STI status and it is not in alignment with yours? Can you respond calmly and sensitively? Will you be rude and dismissive, which would further perpetuate the growing stigmas, myths, and discriminations against people living with these diseases, inadvertently further encouraging these people to keep their diagnosis silent?

Let's say this person potentially meets most of your other requirements. Does this make that person any less of a suitable mate? In some cases that may be a yes, in others maybe a no. Hopefully, before you are met with this question, do your own research to learn about the different STIs and treatments to get an understanding of what you can and cannot live with. This will better prepare you if this issue arises during your dating journey.

Lastly, I advise you to be tested if you have not done so in the last year for your safety and knowledge. Many STIs are completely curable if caught early enough, but when undiagnosed, they can cause permanent damage or issues to your body. Please note that most doctors will not include HIV or Herpes Simplex 1 and 2 tests unless you specifically ask for them. Also, note that Syphilis is back as if we are in the Roaring '20s again, so request to be tested for that, too, if it is not offered to you.

Access Granted

So, you have finally found someone you approve of and are ready to share your body with. There are some things to consider before allowing him in your sacred place. If possible, go to a hotel instead of your home or his. I like to have the upper hand, so I am not too quick to go bouncing my ass over a dude's house. Too many of my friends have experienced situations with the results being another woman knocking on the door and then them having to fight or mean-mug their way out of the house. Awkward.

If you decide to take him to your home, be certain you do not have any lingering exes, boyfriends, or husbands. Most men aren't eager to go over to a woman's house for the same reason previously mentioned. Personally, I don't blame them.

Here is a checklist to make sure you are ready for this huge step:

• You are pretty certain that this man is safe, and you are completely comfortable with him.

• Your children are not home (if you are doing the thang at your place), so you will not have any interruptions, and it is too soon for him to meet them anyway.

• Your house is completely clean, and it smells welcoming. Men will judge you based on how you live, and they should. Even if you are financially challenged, there is no excuse for being untidy. That includes emptying trash cans, dusting, mopping the floor, cleaning, everything. That tub should not have a ring around it, and the toilet should not be stained. You want it to be spotless because, immediately, he will wonder (if he is taking you seriously) what type of life and household you two will have if you were to have a future together.

- He has taken you out on several dates and has invested time and money in you. You are sure at this moment that you want to keep him around. P.S., it's perfectly fine to change your mind later.

- If you decide to sleep with him, you will not pull out all of your best moves on the first encounter. As you grow closer and more comfortable with him, you will reveal yourself like a rose opening to bloom. Your best is to be earned and not given right away. Let him feel that you don't do everything with everybody. Let him feel special when the time is right. But don't do some shit and say, "I never do this." He won't believe you; I wouldn't, either.

- You have asked, or will ask, the tough questions about his sexual health. Are they living with an STI?

- You will ensure enough lighting in your bedroom, or wherever you decide to begin, to look at his penis because there are some things a condom cannot protect you from. If you are grown enough to have sex, be grown enough to look at it. I find that orange Halloween lighting looks good on brown skin and allows enough light to see everything. This is not the time to be shy.

- You will not pull out the box of Magnums in hopes that he can fit them. If he cannot, that will destroy his self-esteem (learned that the hard way). The best practice is for him to have his own, but if you absolutely have to, pull out your condoms. Start with the average sized ones and then move up if necessary. Always keep your own condoms on you and ensure he puts them on correctly.

Now, after that first encounter, things can get serious or completely come to a halt. The probability of the first time being perfect is not likely, but hopefully, it is good enough for you to want to continue moving forward. I like to operate on a three-strikes-you-out deal, but ONLY if the man is batting at a hundred in every other area. Once you enter the sexual stage of the relationship, a few things can happen.

Either he will continue treating you like he was before or better, which means: he will keep doing the things that led to you feeling comfortable enough to open up to him, or he will think that he laid it on you so good that now you are going to start spending your evenings lying around in the bedroom as opposed to going out like you used to.

Don't get me wrong, lying around for hours with a newfound mate can be wonderful, but you do not want to get too comfortable in the relationship too fast. He still needs to continue working to win your **Love**. As most seasoned women know, once a man thinks he has laid it on you, that is when, as my granny used to say, "The peacock will start strutting."

Don't be surprised if that thing called an ego starts rearing its head, and that's perfectly fine; a little head never hurts anybody. Just know that your job is to make sure that homeboy stays consistent.

Be aware that some men will try to secure a casual sexual relationship with you while still pursuing other women. Make it hard for him to do so. It's OK to want to stay in sometimes, but not every weekend. Constantly have something for you guys to do; it does not always have to be expensive, but just enjoyable. As we discussed before, men know what type of woman they want to marry, and if you are considering him long-term, even if he may not be considering you at this time, then you need to make sure he is the type of mate that you feel you can live with, and you want to make sure that it is you who holds the cards.

Again, do not let him get too comfortable too fast, or you may end up in a boring relationship, sitting on the couch all of the time. Since you are still in the dating stages, treat every encounter like a date. When he shows that he is courting you and moving toward a relationship, then you can move some of the other dudes, whether imaginary or not, out the way. I say imaginary because, until he is your man, he does not need to know if you are dating just him.

Now, once you are intimate, and if you both are die-hard monogamous (so you both say), I feel it's OK if he feels you may be only sleeping with him but still go out with whomever you want and not be available 24/7 for him. Most women, when asked, still prefer to sleep with one man at a time. It is usually only when the sex sucks or is not frequent enough that she will venture elsewhere. Men who present semi-hard overly-used penises make it easy for women to move on and find other mates. We can usually tell when they are banging someone else. The best practice is to not eliminate the other potentials until you are both certain that it's a committed relationship.

Living in Love

Oh, to be loved! That euphoric feeling that makes life even more exciting! If you were to Google it, the first definition that may come up is: An intense feeling of deep affection or a great interest and pleasure in something. Love is something that even animals can give and return. It is that thing that everyone ultimately wants, yet it scares us to death. Love can start wars and garner peace. We hear it in our music and see it in our movies. It can be given freely or only acquired through a task. It can be thought of as our most basic birthright, which we have the power to give and receive. It is infinite.

Through life's journey, most of us hopefully will receive some type of love, whether it be the love from our parents or the love from a trusted pet. In terms of romantic love, unfortunately, some will go through this life without truly knowing how it feels. We may even find ourselves in a series of relationships that leave us questioning whether what we were experiencing was true romantic love or its sidekick, infatuation. The problem with love is that everyone does not interpret, give, or receive it the same way. You can only love someone else from the point and understanding of how you have been given and shown love in your own life.

People who grow up without love usually have difficulty experiencing, recognizing, and giving it. Fortunately, in this day and age, there are so many ways that love can be taught that even those who did not have an initial reference point, when coupled with an open partner, can take a love language test to assist them in learning ways that their mate perceives love. Love language tests are just one example of a foolproof way to learn the most basic things that make that special person in your life feel loved and appreciated. But that is just one step in a series of events and moments that you both have to be open to.

As wonderful as romantic love is, self-love is the most powerful form of love. Without self-love, you cannot love anyone else. It is impossible to truly love someone if you are not in a healthy place. Trying to love someone while you are going through turmoil is like trying to pour from an empty cup. When you take care of yourself and are in a healthy space, the love within shines through, and you will attract others because they want what you have.

Sometimes, some of those attractions may not be good for you, and this is when you have to be vigilant in protecting your peace and space. Not everyone deserves your love. It should be given freely while still protected at all costs. If your ultimate goal is to fall in love, get married (or be in partnership), then you have to be extremely careful about who you choose to give your love to. Too many people leave relationships bitter and angry because the love they gave (and/or received) was not reciprocated or was damaging. They vow never to love again, or they make the next person they meet pay for what someone else did. You have to be careful of anyone who thinks you have to prove your love to them or earn their love. These people usually are damaged and unhealed.

Love often comes with expectations, and when those are not always communicated properly to the other party, it tends to fall apart. Always practice good communication in your romantic relationships and work with your partner to keep the love flowing. Being able to express your wants and needs is the foundation for a good partnership. I am a strong believer in loving freely, cautiously, and intentionally. I am careful who I choose to love because my cup is full.

Ever notice those happy couples that have managed to stay together for what seems like forever? Those are the die-hard teams that understand what hard work it takes and have committed to the task of staying together. They have learned how to grow in love as opposed to just falling in love. It is an intentional process that not everyone is up for. Please note that this is not to be confused with a long marriage. As mentioned previously, a long marriage (or committed relationship) does not always equate to a happy one. I would much rather have experienced several long-term relationships that have ended on good terms after giving it our all than to remain in just one miserable one. That is not my idea of success!

Pimpette Chronicles

The truth that no one wants to admit is that not all romantic loves are meant for the entirety of this life. Sometimes we will only be in love with people for a limited amount of time. That does not mean that we will ever stop loving them. Love is not linear and is filled with twists and turns, just like everything else in life. If life was just a straight line, wouldn't it be quite boring? The same concept holds true for love.

As I have grown older, I have learned that everything and everyone has an expiration date. Relationships, like all things in life, truly will have their seasons. It is wise to know when to walk away from love if self-love or respect is the cost. A man who truly loves you will not do anything he knows will harm you. If the love you are in is causing you pain, then it is too high a cost.

"You've got to learn to leave the table, when love is no longer being served." — Nina Simone

The ability to love openly without fear, pain, and regret may always be a challenge, but staying where you are not being loved properly is a threat to your ability to love again. Never let what someone else did to you prevent you from experiencing and giving love. Take those life lessons and move forward wiser and stronger. Living in love is a beautiful thing that I hope, someday, you can grow to achieve.

Photo Credit: Felicia Tolbert, Starpointe Photography. Greg Dimitroff, photography editor.

Special Acknowledgements

My brother, Sean Deason, for always supporting my crazy, creative endeavors over the years: poetry, film festivals, movies, and now a book! You are the best big brother a sister could have!

My mother, Georgia Hickman, for all the love, support, and encouragement over the years. You were also a key player in helping me develop a love for storytelling.

My greatest supporter throughout my life and creative journey, Charrise Bowden. Somehow, you always breathe positivity into me and stand with me during good or bad. You are the MVP!

My friend Robin Clary, for always breathing love and life into me, listening when no one else could hear, and never hesitating to support me in and contribute to my many endeavors.

My eldest daughter, Alicia, who always listens to me, even when you don't understand my reasons. Your compassion and strength push me forward with pride. You are my little friend now!

My youngest daughter Allanah, my Mini-Me. You inspire me to grow and push toward financial freedom. You are all the things I wish I was at your age. You are ahead of the game!

My photographer Felicia Tolbert, for being amongst the first to read my initial rough drafts and encourage me to move forward with this book.

My D.P. Tonya Core, for the kick-ass video trailer and for—rather on purpose or by accident—always providing a different perspective and challenging me to dig deeper.

My Pimp Chronicles Group Members for the engaging and inspiring conversations that ignited my spark of an idea into a flame!

My real life and social media family and friends, for preorders, donations, reposts, and support!

You all are my support system, and I appreciate each one of you.

Be healed. Love well!
Tinisha

A Special Thank You To

Empowering Women Supporter

Kwaku Osei

Pimpette Chronicles Supporters

Tony Braun
Kalisha Davis
Malcolm X. Johnson
Alicia Storm Morales
Isabelle Moses
Abeni Wilson-Williams-Oakman
Susan Norwood
Jeanette Richmond